A TRIP ROUND THE BAY

Recollections of pleasure boats at Rhyl

1936-1967

P.G.C. Longfield

A TRIP ROUND THE BAY

A Trip Round The Bay was first published in Great Britain in August 2011 by Coast & Country Publications, Tyldesley House, Clarence Road, Llandudno, Conwy LL30 1TW.

www.coastandcountrymagazine.co.uk

This paperback edition was first published in August 2011. Text © 2011 P.G.C. Longfield. The Amazon Kindle version was first published online in December 2011.

Front cover designed and illustrated By Nicola Devereux BA, Granddaughter of the Author.

The moral right of P.G.C. Longfield to be identified as author of this work has been asserted by him in accordance with the Copyright, Designs and Patents Act 1988.

All rights reserved. No part of this book may be reproduced or utilized in any form or by any means, electronic or mechanical, including photocopying, recording, or by any information storage or retrieval system, without prior permission in writing from the author and/or the stated publishers.

A catalogue record for this book is available from the British Library.

Paperback edition ISBN 978-1-907163-42-5

Typeset and designed by Katie Gatton BA.

CONTENTS

THE BEACH AND HISTORY OF BOATING	page 1
THE WINTER SEASON	page 10
WINTER PROGRAMME	page 13
CONSTRUCTION OF A NEW JETTY	page 32
THE WORKSHOP	page 36
PICTURES	page 41
THE SUMMER SEASON	page 58
ACKNOWLEDGEMENTS	page 91

This book is dedicated to my late Wife Anna, without whose encouragement it would never have been published.

FOREWORD

In setting out this little book in which I have tried to give an insight into the motor passenger boat industry which once existed in Rhyl, I am aware that there are many gaps, each generation seems reluctant to ask questions about the previous one.

I was as guilty as anyone: There were many questions that I should have asked when there were those around me who could have provided the answers, but now they are gone, and so I can only describe what I can remember, much of it from first hand experience during the period 1936 to 1967 when the last large passenger boat left Rhyl, bringing to an end another chapter in the Town's history.

In a world where changes take place very rapidly, it is perhaps incumbent on those who think that their occupation or way of life could vanish, to make notes, take photographs and record for posterity their unique contribution to our heritage.

Front cover image "May Queen" foreground and "Duke of Edinburgh" approx. date 1950

THE BEACH AND HISTORY OF BOATING

The Beach at Rhyl, as I first remembered it, was much the same as it is today. That is to say that the Training Wall which directs the River Clwyd out to sea, was if not fully in place, sufficiently advanced so as to alter the course of the River from it's bed along the beach and outside the pier, now demolished, to the present day route.

I used to hear the old hands describe how prior to 1935-37 when the Training Wall was built, the beach rose quite steeply from the River, and they had terms for the different sections of the River in which they fished for salmon with nets.

There was the 'run' which is a term still in use today, the 'wild run' and the 'wild wild run' which would be in the area of the Bar, a fearsome place to be in a small rowing boat if the weather was rough.

I recall they also spoke of an area called 'swallow bank'

I shall not dwell on the very early days of pleasure boating, that section of Rhyl's history has been researched and vividly described by D.W. Harris in his book "The Maritime History of Rhyl and Rhuddlan"; suffice to say that the coming of the railway finally put Rhyl on the map as a desirable sea-side resort, although it attracted many visitors to the Town before that date, and local boatmen and fishermen and even the odd entrepreneur were quick to realise the potential. Families would come to Rhyl, very often with their own maids or nannies, and take up residence for a week or two in the many guest houses on the promenade, and I am informed that boat trips were available in sailing boats, before the introduction of engine power.

A little booklet entitled 'Liverpool to North Wales Pleasure Steamers' describes how Rhyl in 1829 enjoyed a daily service of paddle steamers from the resort to Liverpool, departing from the Foryd and later from the pier built in 1867.

My recollections of pleasure boating in Rhyl start around 1936, and by then the small boats carrying possibly twelve persons and working off the beach with a single plank slung from the bow to embark and disembark their passengers had disappeared, with the exception of the "Mayflower". I grew up among passenger boats which were some thirty five to forty foot long and carried between forty and fifty persons, I recall the names, "Duchess of York", "Duke of York", "White Thistle" and "Majestic", some of these vessels were in service long before I arrived on the scene, I have on record that the "White Thistle IV" was built in 1927, the "Duchess of York" 1929 and the "Majestic" 1933.

They were all shallow draughted open boats with a small foredeck for loading purposes and a narrow aft deck on which was stowed the rope and stern anchor. At two points down the length of the boat and the full width of the vessel, were bulkheads about eighteen inches high, to divide the hull into three watertight compartments, these were very necessary constructional features, but presented passengers with a bit of an obstacle race twice every trip. The 'canny' ones tried to sit in the front section, but were always urged to "move right down the boat please".

Most of the boats certainly the "Majestic" had a metal framework over part of the seating area, on which a canvas cover could easily be unrolled, to give shelter from the rain or shade from the sun. These were not completely successful, as they caught a lot of wind, and made handling of the boat more difficult, but the framework was useful for storing the long poles or oars which we used, to hold the boat whilst at the jetty.

The engine was housed in a wooden 'engine box' and was designed to run on petrol and paraffin; for the journey to and from sea the fuel would be paraffin, and whilst idling at the beach the engineer or crew member would switch to petrol to avoid stalling. Needless to say that on a hot day, sitting near the engine box, fairly low down in the hull waiting for the boat to fill up could be a pretty nauseating experience.

With the arrival of the above types of pleasure boats, the method of getting passengers on to them had changed. The beach was quite steep, the effects of the river training wall would make themselves known in later years, and I will refer to this later, and because of this steepness or gradient it was possible to use just one portable jetty of some thirty five to forty feet in length.

The portable jetty took over from the bow loading plank; because the boats were bigger and heavier and as their numbers grew, so they tended to operate from pitches all along the beach to High Street.

In so doing they became susceptible to tide runs, and sometimes choppier conditions on the shore line and needed something substantial to secure to.

With the larger jetties came the horse, and all the relevant problems associated with these huge yet docile animals. How well I remember as a boy, helping to 'round up' our horse from fields in Marsh Road now occupied by Rhydwen Drive; how he knew it was time for work and would gallop round and round the field until we were able to put a bridle on him.

Then came the best part, a ride on his broad and swaying

back over the H bridge and up to the beach. From the maintenance point of view they were the perfect answer, requiring only feed at regular intervals, careful attention to their hooves, and in the Winter turned out to grass on local farms, one I remember being at Llanfair-Talhaiarn. During the summer season he would be stabled in Bridge Street a short walk from the promenade. I was told that whilst in the stable, he was startled by something, prompting a member of the public to rush round to my family home in Palace Avenue shouting "Mr. Hughes, the horse has run away with the stable"! Apparently he had appeared in the street with the stable door round his neck.

The precise problem that they experienced with their feet had always puzzled me, and it was only recently that I was told by a man who owns shire horses, that the salt water removed the natural oils in their skin, and the remedy was to apply at regular intervals to their legs and hooves, pig oil or Stockholm tar or a mixture of both.

Their working day on the beach was quite short and relatively easy compared to working horses on farms, some five or six hours a day with many days off due to bad weather. Once the jetty had been hauled down to the point where the boat would arrive for the first trip that day, and lined up facing the promenade, there was little for the horse to do except for the occasional short pull up the beach as the tide rose; on the ebb the horse would be manoeuvred until it's haunches made contact with the shore end of the jetty and occasional pushes were carried out as the tide receded.

I was told that quite a number of visitors watching the horse at work, thought that it was cruel and that on more than one occasion we were reported to the Authorities. Another complaint was that they thought the horses, because there were several on the beach were a danger to children, although I can never remember anyone being injured.

The only time the horse appeared to find the work heavy was when the outer jetty wheels had settled in the soft wet sand as a result of a long period of standing. Then he would lean forward in his harness, legs straight as he took the strain and broke the jetty out of the holes, and this of course is what would prompt onlookers to say that the animal was being mistreated. In actual fact these were shire horses some sixteen and a half to seventeen and a half hands high, a hand being four inches and the measurement taken from the ground to the withers (shoulders) and weighing in excess of a ton, ideally suited to pulling immense weights.

Between work periods, he could be seen standing quietly by the jetty eating a well earned meal from his feed bag.

The small single screw passenger boat continued to operate through the thirties, and then in 1937 my Uncle Mr T.J. (Jack) Hughes commissioned Crossfields of Conwy to build him a fifty foot twin screw decked passenger boat which was given the name "Queen Elizabeth". She was a great improvement on the open boats, passengers now found that they could move freely about the deck, and although she had a raised deck section amidships to give height to the engine room; yes we now enjoyed the luxury of an engine room as distinct from an engine box, this did not present anything like the problem experienced with the open boat bulkheads.

Now the passengers sat above the water with a good all round view, no engine fumes, just the fresh sea breezes in their faces. From the operational aspect there was an immediate improvement in turn around time at the jetty as passengers flowed on and off, and I am sure that the disabled and elderly appreciated this new facility.

Something else became available as the result of having a decked boat, and that was music; I vaguely remember a harpist who pushed his harp around on an old pram, playing on the after deck accompanied by a young boy on the violin. If I recall correctly this was only for a short period, regular music on the boats was still some years away.

I am writing about events as if I spent every day on the boat, in actual fact I was only nine when the "Queen Elizabeth" came to Rhyl, but I spent as much time on the beach near the boats as I could, when not in school, which happened to be in Prestatyn, and on more than one occasion whilst waiting for a bus at the top of High Street, the lure of the sea was too much for me, the boat was at the jetty about to leave, so I jumped aboard and played truant.

This for someone who a year or two earlier had waited for the boat to cast off and then screamed to be put ashore, much to the annoyance of my Uncle.

Such was the success of the "Queen Elizabeth" and no doubt encouraged by good seasons, my Uncle decided to place an order, again with Crossfields to build him another passenger vessel.

This one was to surpass all the others both in size and carrying capacity, she was sixty feet in length with a beam of seventeen feet, and passed by the Board of Trade to carry one hundred and fifteen passengers, and yet like all Crossfield boats she only had a draught of two feet six inches fully laden. Whilst on the subject of passenger carrying capacity, I was in touch with the MCA (Maritime Coastguard Service) at Falmouth, where the "May

Queen" is now working, and they have on file, some seventy two years later, a letter from Crossfields dated 1939,of which I now have a copy, in which they express disappointment with the then Board of Trade for initially allowing one hundred and thirty seats, then reducing the number to one hundred and twenty. The final seating figure as mentioned above turned out to be one hundred and fifteen. Work began in 1939 and I remember as a boy going to Conwy to see her grow in size week by week, from a single length of local Welsh oak for the keel, to a skeleton of grown oak frames and ribs, upon which were steamed and fastened inch and one eighth thick pitchpine planks

Once at this stage of construction, she filled the long narrow shed which dominated Crossfield's boat yard, which nestled against the seaward side of the old town wall where it ends by the archway which leads onto the promenade area famous for the "Smallest House"; Welsh Water now occupy the boatyard site.

I had a very interesting conversation with Mr. Vincent Crossfield who had helped to build the 'May Queen' as she came to be called, back in 1939. He surprised me by saying that they had very little in the way of machinery, each piece of timber was hand worked with adzes, draw knives and planes, and yet despite this, he informed me that four men built her in six weeks.

With the success of decked passenger vessels, a new pattern was starting to emerge on the boating scene, but the onset of World War Two brought things to a temporary halt.

The "May Queen" brand new from the builders in September 1939 was commandeered by the Government and spent the war years as a fire fighting tender on the River Mersey at Liverpool, and was not involved in the evacuation of Dunkirk as was the impression of many people after the war. I was told that the authorities instructed my Uncle to break up the winter bed the "May Queen" was on, so that she could be used immediately.

It had, been my intention to write a chapter entitled "The War Years," but my failing to ask enough questions at the time, means that my knowledge of what happened is extremely vague, and would not warrant a separate section, I do know that the above commissioning took place, but it seems that my Uncle still had the "Queen Elizabeth", something I was not aware of, until I took a trip to Fleetwood, where I knew that she finished up, but what surprised me was the date she actually arrived there. In the Public Library I found an account of vessels used on the Knott End ferry, and I quote the first paragraph.

"In 1941, after the sale of the small well-type vessel "Pilling" the "Caldervale" was bought second-hand for £2000 from her Rhyl owners. A decked shallow draught vessel, she was built in Conwy, North Wales in 1937, having twin American Atlantic engines (petrol Paraffin type) of 30H.P. each."

The significance is the year 1941, it is obviously the "Queen Elizabeth" re-named, so did the Authorities allow my Uncle to keep one boat, so as not to deprive him of any kind of a livelihood, and did people come on holiday during the early days of the war?, perhaps he held on to the boat, hoping as we all did that the war would be short lived. This I confess I do not know, but it is a fact that at some stage, access to the beach from the sea would have been impossible, due to the hundreds of poles set in the sand to prevent enemy invasion forces from landing. The Government also issued the advice to boat owners, to take the engine starting handles ashore when leaving vessels in the harbour, this would of course include fishing boats that could probably carry on fishing during the war years.

Rhyl was certainly a very different town after war broke out, many people moved from the cities to the comparative safety of the coast, evacuees were brought into town, and many of the large hotels and boarding houses were commandeered by the Government, also a large number of soldiers were billeted in Rhyl, and as the war progressed many Americans added to the numbers.

Thus we have my entire knowledge of events at that time, how I wish now I had taken more interest, but I was only eleven when war broke out, and I did not ask enough questions, but I must have asked some later, or this little book would never have been written. I do know that when the War ended the "May Queen" looked a sorry sight, the pitchpine hull planks resplendent in many coats of varnish when she left Rhyl in 1939 were now painted black, and the deck had numerous holes in it as a result of the pumps, which had been installed for fire fighting purposes.

At Government expense she was returned to the builders at Conwy, where she was restored as near as possible to her former glory, and the following year the passenger boat business at Rhyl started up again.

THE WINTER SEASON

I was often asked the question "what do you find to do all winter?" or, "I suppose you have got the winter off now?" the inference being in some cases that we made enough money during the summer season, and therefore had no need to work during the winter. In theory one could be forgiven for thinking that way, as seaside towns can usually provide a considerable number of seasonal jobs but precious little in the winter, and many people have the winter off though not of their own choosing, indeed if we had a bad season with the boats, there followed a very lean winter.

In the earlier years of pleasure boating when boats were small and beach equipment no more than a plank or single jetty, once the boat had been secured on it's winter bed, and the horse as the case may be had gone to winter grazing, there was indeed much spare time until Easter the following year, heralded the start of another season. Much of this spare time was taken up in shrimping or fishing, I can recall several occasions when as a boy I had accompanied my Uncle as we trawled up and down outside Rhyl for shrimps and other species of fish, and here I must confess is where I suffered my first and only encounter with seasickness, brought on no doubt by the endless rolling as we slowly moved parallel to the shore, and from the fumes from the exhaust pipe which always seemed to exit from the side of the boat and consequently very often were carried inboard by the wind.

The situation began to change as the pleasure boats began to increase in size, from open boats some thirty five to forty feet in length, to decked boats fifty to sixty feet long, single screw was replaced by twin screw, and all the while as the levels of the beach deteriorated so additional jetties were required, and the willing horse was replaced by tractors.

This expansion of the motor boat industry now meant that come the end of the summer season there was a quite considerable amount of maintenance and repair work to be carried out, and here one must remember that given anything like an average summer the best days had been spent working and now winter was approaching, many of the jobs to be done were outside, consequently there were quite a few 'lost' days due to bad weather.

My entry into the boating business on a full time basis came in 1947 when along with my Uncle Mr. Stanley Edwards we joined my Uncle Mr. T.J.Hughes who at that stage was seriously considering giving up, partly for health reasons, and also because as already indicated the work load was becoming quite demanding, and gone were the days when casual labour could be relied on to carry out the many odd jobs that cropped up. I had spent two and a half years prior to 1947 as an apprentice motor mechanic at the White Rose Garage, now the White Rose Shopping Precinct and had come to the conclusion that another two and a half years of grime and sweat was not a price I wanted to pay, to qualify for what in those days was a very poorly paid profession, but I was soon to realize how useful the knowledge that I had already acquired would prove to be in my new career.

In saying that there was considerable work to be done during the winter, one could not pretend to say that we worked long hours every day, indeed we started in the morning at a very reasonable hour and in the short days of winter we finished early, but we always kept an eye on the calendar, for an early Easter could easily catch you unprepared and we always worked to some kind of a timetable. It can be argued that the more time you have, the longer a job can take, and in later years as I took on family responsibilities I was of necessity forced to seek other work during the winter months, this took the form in the earlier years, of landscape gardening with a Mr. Sid Hole who had a nursery at the end of Avondale Drive off Dyserth Road , for whom I worked mornings only, which meant that I could devote the rest of the day to cleaning out bilges or caulking decks or whatever was current on our endless list of jobs at the Foryd.

In later years after a succession of poor summers I was fortunate enough to obtain employment with Arthur Hapgood Shopfitters who at that time had their yard and workshops in Sussex Lane behind the Baptist Chapel, and who were kind enough to allow me to work the winter months with them and return to the boating activities for the summer.

This arrangement worked very well I like to think for both sides, they had contracts which required extra labour and here was I learning a new set of skills which could be brought to bear on the tasks which arose in the Harbour; the only problem was that virtually all of my spare time, week-ends and even some evenings, when we could set up work in our workshop, was fully occupied in still trying to meet the Easter deadline.

I keep referring to the amount of work which had to be carried out during the winter months, so I feel I should take the reader through a typical winter programme to show what went on behind the scenes to prepare for the day when the pleasure boat, resplendent in gleaming new paintwork and be-decked with new bunting arrived on the beach for that first trip of the summer season.

WINTER PROGRAMME

In any normal season we would hope to run trips around the bay until the third week in September, indeed I have seen Mr. Todd operating the "'White Thistle" from opposite High Street as late into the season as the second week in October, if we happened to be blessed with an 'Indian Summer.' We were also fortunate in those days to have a very enterprising publicity officer who promoted and encouraged early and late holidays for old age pensioners as they were called in those days, before they all, including myself were promoted to the rank of senior citizens.

As a result , once the children had gone back to school for the Autumn term, you would find us ,weather permitting leaving the beach with some hundred plus passengers, with ages ranging from sixty five onwards, who had all braved the long beach ramps, the hundred and fifty feet of jetties, and the step onto a deck which had a nasty habit of moving up and down on some days; but how they loved those half hour cruises, a calm sea and a chance to sing along with Tony Ward and his accordion to the old favourites 'Daisy' and 'Lily of Laguna' One thing I could never fail to notice was that some seventy five per cent of those passengers were women, and I always used to wonder with some foreboding "what had happened to the men?"

Season over, our first job was to remove all the loose equipment from the boat, masts were taken down, lifebelts and buoyancy seats removed and stored in our workshop. Next came the inspection of the winter berth which took the form of ex. railway sleepers secured to the ground by wooden or steel pegs, or if the contour of the bank would allow, the sleepers were set on concrete pillars to provide easier access to the underpart of the boat's hull.

Over the years the passenger boats had various winter homes, I seem to remember as a young boy seeing some laid up on the marsh bank in front of the present Yacht Club. The "May Queen" for many years was on a bed which I had a hand in building which was just alongside the boundary wall of Harry Fielding's cottage as it was known then, it's actual name was 'Langford', and which later became the home of a local builder who had as his workshop the old lifeboat house which was in commission from 1867 to 1899 and which also shared the site in Old Foryd Road; this building is sadly no longer in existence.

How well I remember as a boy climbing over the ivy covered wall into the garden and wandering around the semi-derelict bungalow, I seem to remember that it was boarded up because I cannot recall that I went inside. One memory that has stayed with me over the years is of a large yellow glass knob on the front door, which to my boyish mind looked as if it might have been extremely valuable.

The inspection of the bed complete, and any necessary repairs having been carried out, we were almost ready to bring the boat through from the summer moorings in the harbour, but the final task usually carried out the day before moving her, was to transport round to the winter bed site, two lengths of chain and two extremely large and heavy anchors. These were set out at an angle of forty five degrees from a point where the bow of the boat would eventually finish up, and connected together at the pick up point with a short length of rope and a buoy. At the opposite end of the bed we laid out a much lighter temporary rope mooring which we could quickly take in over the stern. Finally we fastened a wooden batten to the centre support on the bed which was marked in feet and inches to enable us to gauge exactly how much water would be over the bed.

At this point perhaps I should explain that a great deal of care and thought had to be given to the construction of a winter mooring bed if it was to be one hundred per cent efficient, certainly the one we used for many years worked very well, because we had achieved a satisfactory height for the bed in relation to the tidal range we experience on this part of the coast. To explain further, we have 'neap' tides which give relatively small watermarks and largely go unnoticed, and 'spring ' tides which contrary to popular belief do not occur only in the spring but produce twice a month, tides which give higher watermarks. Thus we have a range of tides from the small 22'-0" up to as high as 33'-0" or 6.7 metres to 10 metres, these figures based on a datum level at Liverpool from which we locals always deducted 10'-0" or 3 metres to obtain a local datum.

I have deliberately gone into a detailed explanation of local tides because it helps the reader to realize that to allow the boat hull to stay dry for long periods to enable us to carry out such tasks as caulking of seams and painting, she, and boats are always referred to in the feminine gender, had to be berthed as high as possible, but not so high that she could fail to re-float in the Spring should the required tide at that time fail to reach it's predicted height. This may sound a strange thing to say in the light of present day technology, but weather conditions have a very real effect on tide levels. Strong winds in the South to West quadrant, and depressions approaching from the West can produce tides much higher than predicted, conversely winds from the North and East can greatly reduce the predicted tide height.

I can recall several years when cold Easterly winds set in during March, the month when we usually moved the boat off the winter bed, and we spent anxious moments watching the tide slowly creep up, fall short of it's predicted height , but provide us with a few brief moments to haul the boat off the bed, when we should have had ample time and water.

On the day chosen to move to winter moorings, and having sent suitable prayers aloft for a calm day we would be aboard at the first touch of the incoming tide, and as soon as there was sufficient water we would move through the harbour and pass under the Foryd Bridge, before the tide rip set in and whilst we still had clearance under the bridge. Once through we would anchor up in the relatively slack water between the old toll house stone abutment and the bridge, and sit out the two and a half hours up to high water, breaking the time up with the occasional walk to the bed to check the progress of the incoming tide against our depth gauge. Just before high water we would start our final approach to the bed inching into position over it, not for us the luxury of tugs, and securing to the moorings laid out the previous day, knowing that very soon the boat would settle on the sleeper bed on the already turned tide.

Once we were satisfied that the hull had settled firmly on the bed, it was home for a quick bite to eat and then back to the harbour to tackle what was probably the most unpleasant task in the entire boating calendar; scraping the barnacles off the bottom.

As the summer season progressed we would notice the boat's passage through the water becoming more and more laboured, a problem only partly remedied by increasing the throttle settings, the reason for this being as we were well aware, the ever increasing growth of barnacles on the underwater surfaces of the hull. As all the passenger boats which worked from Rhyl beach were specially designed to have very shallow draught, it was impossible to reach very far under the hull, thus we had to be content with a cursory scrape and brush along the water line, until such time that the boat was on the winter bed. So here we were, armed with scrapers and garden hoes flat on our backs, our faces almost touching the hull, scraping off the seasons growth of barnacles, trying to work our way along from the keel out, and as the "May Queen" had a beam of seventeen feet we were some eight feet under the hull inching our way on a piece of board, coated in mud and wet barnacles, our hands covered in scratches from contact with them, but most of all we were subjected to the most foul and nauseating stench of what I would describe as rotting fish.

It always amazed me how tenacious a creature is the barnacle, which starts out in life independent, active and able to swim about, but soon fastens on any surface it can find, where it develops a lime like shell with a moveable lid. It continues to feed whilst attached to a rock or a ship's hull by means of six pairs of feathery feet which wave food into it's mouth. At the base of the shell is a cement gland which provides the 'sticking' quality, so powerful that the barnacle is able to attach itself to such objects as propellers, or stainless steel propeller shafts and is quite happy to stay there even though it's 'home' is revolving at several hundred revolutions a minute.

Perhaps by now the reader is wondering why we were so eager to tackle such a distasteful task on what had been an already busy day, when the whole winter stretched ahead of us. There were two good reasons; firstly if the barnacles were allowed to dry they would take on the constituency of concrete and great physical effort would be necessary to remove them, secondly if we removed them on the first day, the tides which had enabled us to put the boat on it's winter bed would still be high enough for several days to disperse the barnacle shells, thus removing the unpleasant smell.

The scraping job over, all that remained for us to do was to set out chains and anchors at an angle of forty five degrees at the bow, ropes from the stern, these combined with spring ropes, all to ensure that the boat stayed exactly on the centre of the bed. Thus we came to the end of a long day and the "May Queen" settled down for the long winter ahead.

At this time of the year I usually prepared a list of the jobs that needed to be carried out during the six months that lay ahead, this was partly done to ensure that on looking down the list we could order any materials or parts in good time that might be required for a particular job, and also because there was a wonderful sense of order and achievement when a job could be ticked off the list. There was a down side to this system as some outside jobs could drag on for weeks due to adverse weather conditions, and despite all the planning we usually found that several jobs were on the go at the same time all partially completed; I was never happy with this situation, it being in my nature to always complete one task before starting another, but with the occupation I had chosen and the vagaries of our climate I slowly came to accept the situation. I have decided at this point to set out a typical list of tasks which required carrying out in any one winter, and explain in more detail further on what was entailed.

Remove all jetty wheels, clean and re-grease bearings and re-assemble

Replace brake shoes, sprockets and tracks to tractor

Make new portable ramps

Strip, test and re-rope buoyancy raft

Repairs to life rings

Clean out and re-paint bilges on boat

Remove fuel tanks for inspection

Remove propeller shafts and replace stern bearings

Rake out and re-caulk deck and hull where required

Completely strip one engine for Board of Trade inspection

Repairs to jetties

In addition to the list, we occasionally were faced with the construction of a completely new jetty, a task which took several weeks. Also every spring the boat was completely re-painted from mast top to keel.

The fact that work to the jetty wheels was top of the maintenance list was deliberate. Next to barnacle removing, this was the second most urgent task. All summer these wheels, twelve in number, had been immersed in a mixture of sand and salt water, not the sort of ingredients to maintain the performance of roller bearings, and certainly far in excess of the conditions faced on the average motor car, thus we would set about removing all the wheels, washing in petrol all the bearings, re-placing where necessary, cleaning out the sludgy mixture of sand and grease from the hubs and re-packing with fresh grease. Once the wheels had been re-placed, with all the studs and nuts cleaned and liberally coated with grease; for to operate one season without this precaution would have rendered removal of the wheels impossible such was the effect of salt water; the jetties were jacked up on to blocks or baulks of timber to preserve the tyres.

To enable the jetties to be manoeuvred when in use, the inshore set of wheels was secured to a carriage very often salvaged from old horse drawn carts, relics of bygone days testimony to the skills of the wheelwright with adzed edges to the beautifully shaped bars forming the frame, combined with the blacksmiths ability to produce two circular rings to form the turntable, rather like the present day articulated lorry principle. It was these two rings that also needed our attention, a good clean and plenty of grease would simplify a mans' work when the season started.

Next on the list was the tractor used for towing the jetties. I must explain here that I am describing the scenario in which I was mostly involved, the earlier days would have seen as referred to earlier, a shire horse in use to haul the jetties, I was unfortunately presented with the mechanical age, and with the end of the Second World War came the opportunity to purchase Bren Gun Carriers. These were obtained from Government sales or scrap dealers, they were tracked vehicles, powered by Ford V eight engines and steering was implemented by the use of rods and levers connected to the steering wheel which applied the brakes and slewed the vehicle left or right as required by the driver. There were occasions when the brakes were not as efficient as they should have been, I recall that a carrier, the owner shall remain nameless, on it's way to the beach, virtually demolished a tubular support that carried a string of illuminations on the promenade. How many of us were licensed to drive tracked vehicles I never knew, I certainly was not, and when I decided to legalise the situation, there was no one to test me.

Teddy Todd had a Loyd Carrier, a vehicle very similar to the Bren Gun carrier, the difference being that it was steered by two levers, rather than a steering wheel.

It was vital that the steering linkages on all these vehicles were kept well greased, if they were allowed to seize, which could happen within two days if the carrier was not used, as was the case on rough days when trips off the beach were not possible, considerable work was needed to free them off. This task of maintaining the brakes was probably one of our most irksome, often after a lucky spell of good working weather we would long for a day off, but there were always the brakes demanding attention. We did discover a useful idea which I have to admit we gleaned from our then competitors, which was to fit bed springs taken from the angle iron and wire mesh bed frames popular at that time and always on offer at local tips. These springs connected three in line, pulled the linkages back thereby reducing the risk of seizing.

The brakes were only one of the problems associated with the carriers, as mentioned before, they were tracked vehicles and the tracks were driven by sprockets, large toothed rings secured by some twenty odd bolts to the brake drums. The constant abrasive action of the sand reduced the teeth on these sprockets to needle sharp points, the tracks which were links secured by hardened pins also were stretched to the point where a sharp turn by the carrier would cause it to immediately shed a track

By now the reader will have gathered that brake shoes, sprockets and tracks were pretty high on our list of necessary spares, and so most winters we would take a few days off and tour the various dealers yards in order to replenish our stock.

Uncle Stan and I frequently found oureslves lying flat on our backs on a January day in such places as Frodsham or Derby, splitting tracks up into convenient lengths for ease of handling, removing sprockets with their twenty odd often very rusty bolts and nuts, and salvaging brake shoes if still serviceable. Once we had agreed a price with the dealer, the items would be transported to the nearest railway goods depot and in the course of a few days would arrive at Rhyl station to await our collection, this way a corner of our workshop in the Foryd would always have a huge pile of tracks and many sets of sprocket rings, for to be without this stockpile meant the possibility of losing working days in the summer so dependent were we on the beach tractors.

Eventually the supply of bren gun carriers began to dry up, and as a result the prices began to rise sharply, so we turned our attention to ex. Army Quads, these were four wheel drive vehicles which had a very powerful winch operated through the gearbox.

I seem to remember that we had one vehicle manufactured by Guy Motors, and a later one which was a Morris. The Quads greatly reduced our winter maintenance, they had large conventional tyred wheels, and the inclusion of a winch meant that the vehicle was never immersed in the sea, as was the case with the bren carriers.

The decision to use these quads was not without a certain amount of trial and error. I recall going with my Uncle to a sale of surplus army vehicles at Ruddington near Nottingham, where a huge array of equipment was on view. I was personally interested in making a bid for some ex staff cars which in those days were Hillman Minx, some with very low mileage, but I recall that bids soon reached £400 to £500 which seemed to me at the time to be astronomical.

We did however purchase a Crossley Prime Mover, a huge vehicle on four enormous tyres, which we thought would cope with the softest of sands, so we duly brought it back to Rhyl, where we found that it had an insatiable appetite for petrol, in fact the carburettor would consume petrol as fast as one could pour it into it's huge bowl. Worse than that we quickly became aware of a problem that had not occurred to any of us at the time of purchase, which was that the front wheelbase was narrower than the rear, with the result that instead of the front wheels making a track in the sand in which the rear wheels could follow, each set of wheels had to cut their own passage, which meant that the vehicle soon became bogged down in the very soft parts of the beach.

So we learnt our lesson the hard way, but thanks to the kindness of Mr. J. S. Jones who was a public works contractor, and who had taken us to the auction, and who said he had a use for it, we were able to dispose of the 'monster' quite quickly. Now with greater experience we bought a Quad which proved ideal for the work.

I referred earlier to 'lost days,' those times when rain or severe cold forced us into the workshop, giving us a chance to tackle some of the lighter items of work on our list, chief of these was the maintenance of the buoyancy seats. In order to comply with what was the Board of Trade, now the MCA (Maritime Coastguard Agency), the "May Queen" had to carry life rafts capable of supporting 108 persons, these consisted of three base units and three back to back seat units, one seat to sit on one base. Inside the bases and seats were copper tanks, three to each which gave the buoyancy, and around each seat and base were loops of rope, each loop having a wooden toggle.

In theory, should the boat ever have been in imminent risk of sinking, we as crew were supposed to get the rafts in the sea, and instruct the passengers to enter the water as calmly as possible and use the rafts for support, by putting one arm through the rope loops. When questioned by passengers as to their use, it became obvious that the majority were under the impression that they could sit on the seat units. In actual fact I always felt that in an emergency that is exactly what would have happened, as it would take some courage especially if you were a non- swimmer to be up to your neck in the sea with just a loop of rope to hang on to.

It goes without saying that this was a scenario I did not wish to dwell on for too long.

Regulations demanded that one third of these rafts were inspected every year, and we got into the routine of removing six tanks and cutting off the old ropes to two rafts. Then would begin the task of threading the end of the new rope through the timber side rail on the raft and passing it through one strand of the rope at regular intervals to form the loops, remembering always to place a toggle on the loop before passing on. This was a procedure that became easier as the length of rope to be pulled through the strands got steadily shorter all the time. When the two ends of the rope met they were finished with a short splice.

The tanks had to be tested for any cracks or holes that might have occurred along the soldered seams, and here we were fortunate in as much that the Council decided to upgrade the derelict triangular piece of land between Wellington Road and the Promenade, and incorporated a circular boating pool. This being only about twelve inches deep was ideal, as Uncle Stan and myself could stand in the pool and force the tanks under the water in order to look for tell tale bubbles which indicated a leak. Once we were satisfied, the rafts were re-assembled and date stamped.

The remaining buoyancy aids which provided full cover to the 115 passengers we were licensed to carry, were life rings, these were of cork construction covered in canvas with lines attached at four points by heavier canvas strips. Occasionally we would be inspected by an over zealous Board of Trade surveyor who would subject the lines to what I always felt were forces that would not arise in normal use, and so we would be left with the task of getting some bands of very stiff canvas made up by the local cobbler, for the sewing of the edges was too heavy a job for the average domestic sewing machine.

Once ready I recall spending much time armed with a sail-makers needle, waxed thread and a sail-makers palm, sewing the bands on to the life-rings. The sail-makers palm is worthy of a brief mention as I am sure not too many are seen nowadays. It was basically a narrow leather strap widening slightly in the palm area, with a hole to push the thumb through. Between the thumb and first finger and located in the palm area of the hand was a metal disc set in a leather mount with several drilled holes. Once the needle had been positioned in the canvas the eye was located in one of the drilled holes and great pressure could be exerted with safety to push the needle through the folds of canvas and complete the stitch.

When recalling this particular maintenance task, I think how being self-employed, having your own little empire so to speak, gave you such enthusiasm for the job in hand, so much so that I would often go up to the workshop of an evening to potter about, finishing a little job not completed that day, but which could easily have waited until the following morning. Who would do that for a boss?

This dedication to the work led me once to bring home some red paint with the intention of re-painting the bands on the life-rings, in the comfort of my dining room, where I promptly spilt the paint on the carpet. That put an immediate end to any further over-zealous ideas like that.

Another very important winter job was to remove the propellers and propeller shafts. This was done partly because bronze propellers were an expensive item and could easily disappear, although in those days this was not the problem which exists today, sad to say that any boat beached nowadays and not attended to right away, would soon be parted from it's 'prop'. The main reason however was to 'draw' the shafts and examine for wear in the area of the bearings, one such bearing would be in the hull behind what was called the 'stuffing box' and gave very little trouble, but at the propeller end the bearing had been subjected to the abrasive mixture of water and sand which had encouraged wear. On the "May Queen" the original shafts were bronze running in white metal bearings and frequent replacement of both shafts and bearings was necessary.

I had the bright idea of fitting copper pipes from the deck to the bearings and pushing grease through, via a grease gun. This produced a compound akin to valve grinding paste and the idea was soon dropped. In later years we changed to stainless steel shafts, cut back the stern tubes and fitted 'cutless' rubber bearings, which were of bronze construction with a fluted rubber lining which allowed the water to pass through, thus washing the sand out and greatly reducing wear.

Once the shafts and bearings were to our satisfaction, and in the era of bronze shafts and white metal bearings, this could have meant our calling on the services of Crowthers of Manchester, a very old and reliable firm, who would build up and turn the worn shafts, re-balance the propellers, make new stern bearings, and set us up for the next season, when the whole of the stern gear would form part of the Board of Trade survey.

Another important part of the winter work programme was to inspect the underwater planks of the hull, to check that the seams were intact. In wooden boats there are two principal methods of construction, clinker built where the planks are secured to the frames with an overlap to give a stepped effect, and carvel built where the planks butt together to give a smooth hull, as was the case with the "May Queen" and the majority of the other boats. In construction the edges of the planks would be cut on a bevel which meant that when nailed together on the frames they left a vee shaped gap into which caulking cotton and putty was applied.

Because the boats which worked off the beach had to be of shallow draught and of good beam to maximise passenger capacity, they were virtually flat below the waterline, and although extremely stable, on choppy water they had a tendency to pound on the waves and flex which would cause the caulking to 'spew' out of the seams. If our inspection revealed any sign of trouble we used to engage the services of Mr. Tony Hodsoll the local boatbuilder, for re-caulking a boat was a job best left to professionals.

Before anything could be done however the bilges had to be thoroughly dry and we used this opportunity to remove the foul mixture of oil, water and sand that always seems to exist in the bottom of boats. We would first bale into buckets as much as possible and then mop up the dregs with cloths, a slow and tedious task and in winter tough on the hands, in extreme weather I have known the bilges to freeze despite the oil content in them. Once dry, suspect seams were raked out and the re-caulking process could begin.

The strands of caulking cotton were spun up to make a rope appropriate for the seam size, and this was tapped lightly into the seam using a caulking iron into a series of small tucks and then hammered home with the caulking mallet. This tool resembled a croquet mallet, the head was large, approximately twelve to fifteen inches in length, but the shaft was quite short. To anyone who had never seen a boat being caulked they could be forgiven for thinking that the long swing of the mallet and the force behind each blow would split the planks asunder, in reality the mallet head was designed to absorb some of the impact, whilst the shipwright knew from experience the amount of force to apply.

In the wrong hands a badly caulked boat would prove to be a constant source of trouble, the cotton would either fall out within a very short space of time, planks could be split, or sound seams opened up. Although we possessed a mallet and full set of irons we were always reluctant to tackle this particular work.

The practise of putting bevels on the planks and filling the subsequent gaps with cotton etc. was also applied to the deck planks. Here the caulking cotton was covered in pitch and most Springs on a warm and windless day would find us boiling blocks of pitch on a primus stove and running the molten liquid along the seams using a thin spouted ladle, a procedure which called for a steady hand and was rather tedious. The deck planks were only some two and a half inches wide, and I calculated that attention to the entire deck on a vessel the size of the "May Queen" would have involved some four and a half to five thousand feet of seams. Once the pitch was dry, any surplus would be scraped off, and a coat of linseed oil applied to the entire deck.

I have referred earlier to the fact that we were very much under the supervision of the Board of Trade who carried out a survey of the hull and machinery every Spring, followed by our sea trials soon after. To comply with their requirements I and Uncle Stan had to completely dismantle alternate engines each year to enable the surveyor to examine valves, pistons etc, which to us seemed ludicrous, diesel engines are capable of operating for many hundreds of hours without trouble, we in an average season would log some two hundred hours, and we always felt that we did more harm than good in disturbing seals and rings, but such was the ruling and we had to abide by it.

Some of this work involved several back breaking days in the engine room, but we were able to transport the heavy cylinder heads to our workshop and enjoy some time in comfort removing carbon and re-grinding valves.

There was one occasion when our reluctance to disturb the engines unnecessarily seemed justified, it happened as we were re-assembling the starboard engine, we failed to notice that a long push rod was not properly located with the result that on turning the engine over we damaged the cup that the rod sat in. It became obvious that to replace the cup we would have to remove the gearbox and flywheel in order to withdraw the camshaft.

To remove the flywheel we had to contact Listers of Dursley in Gloucestershire the engine manufacturers who sent us in a packing case a huge spanner to tackle the nut on the flywheel. Once the nut was removed we had to rig a dummy shaft onto which we eased the 270 lb. flywheel, withdraw the camshaft and replace the damaged tappet cup, and reassemble the engine, all in the cramped confines of the engine room. If ever the saying "if it ain't broke don't fix it" was applicable it was then.

The only good thing to be said about this episode, is that it happened out of season, but we did experience a gearbox failure during one summer, which meant the removal of same, a frantic phone call to Listers of Dursley in Gloucestershire, to ascertain the spare part situation, a long drive to collect, the return journey, and by working through the night, we were in business the following day. Thus were the uncertainties of our summer season, when everything else took second place.

Another fairly major but necessary task springs to mind. We found rot in the deck beam which served as a fixing for the bulkhead between the engine room and the aft compartment, but only accessible from the engine room. Without taking up some of the deck, this meant that we had to split and chop by hand and remove the offending beam which also passed through two partitions in the engine room, de-nail the deck and partition fixings, and prepare for a replacement beam.

For this task, as with the caulking, we called on Mr. Tony Hodsoll and his assistant Mr. Gerald Hughes who took careful templates and produced a new deck beam in two pieces, joined in the middle with a long scarfed joint, this being the only way to manoeuvre it into position. Needless to say, once in place the fit and the joint were perfect, such was Tony's skill as a boatbuilder.

. Transport in those days was not something we came to expect, the Bren Carriers were not suitable, and the Quads had been mothballed for winter and were not strictly legal on the road, certainly not in the Town. I had no car and both my Uncle Stan and I rode bicycles, and I well remember struggling to get to the Foryd twice a day against the prevailing South Westerly wind which always seemed to be blowing. I invested in a Cyclemaster, a motorized pushbike off which at regular intervals fell various mechanical bits, and the rear wheel constantly needed re-alignment. Needless to say I soon returned to pedal power.

One winter maintenance job springs to mind which illustrates how we coped without motor transport. It became necessary to renew the exhaust system on the "May Queen", a task which entailed removing the old silencers and steel exhaust pipes and providing new, these pipes were some twenty feet in length with bends and flanges screwed on the each end.

We were able to purchase the new pipes from the Water Board Yard which was in Paradise Street, who also had the large stocks and dies necessary to cut threads on the pipes, so for several days my Uncle and I could be seen walking between the Foryd and Town each pushing our bicycles some twenty feet apart supporting the ends of a three inch diameter steel pipe on our handlebars, having taken what we hoped were precise measurements on the boat.

Two thoughts came to me out of this episode; firstly, how easy now to arrange transport, and secondly, how difficult to find such a local personal service in these days of privatisation.

CONSTRUCTION OF A NEW JETTY

I think by now the reader will have a fair idea of the varied tasks on our winter programme, as I mentioned earlier, every few years we were faced with the additional task of making a new landing stage or jetty as we called them.

The little twenty foot ramps, light enough to be handled by two men were easy enough to make, two sides of nine inch by one inch timber with seven inch by one inch spacers, the odd tie rod and some tongue and groove boards laid diagonally for the deck, was all that was needed, a nice little job for the workshop on a rainy day. The portable jetty was a different proposition.

The side timbers were selected from what in the timber trade is called 'clear and best' Douglas Fir or Columbian Pine as some know it. This grade would guarantee a knot free plank; why knot free? To answer this, one has to realize that the timbers were unsupported between the front and rear wheels over a length of some forty feet, and with the added weight of perhaps twenty passengers they would sag quite noticeably, and any knots would immediately weaken the side timbers.

So we would set out to construct a jetty, fifty foot in length, and for this we would purchase two forty foot lengths of twelve inch by two inch Douglas fir, and four twelve foot lengths of the same dimension. These would be laid out on edge on several trestles, each side having a forty foot and twelve foot length, butted together to give the desired fifty two foot finished length. Either side of the butt joints we would position on the inside face, the remaining two twelve foot lengths to over lap the butt joints equally, these were in effect "splints" which would be clamped in position ready for holes to be drilled for the fixing bolts.

The position for the boltholes would be carefully marked out on the outside faces of the side members, usually twenty-four per side, but there was no hard and fast rule, as long as we realized the importance of retaining the strength and not indulged in boring too many holes. This latter situation was not likely to happen as the holes were bored by hand using a carpenter's brace and 5/8"auger bit. It was hard work, I think we had electricity in the workshop at that time, but we possessed very little in the form of extension leads and power tools.

There was some how a great deal of satisfaction in completing a particular task by sheer muscle power and the sweat of the brow, indeed looking back I recall that most jobs were done by hand, cutting threads on rods, scraping off old varnish, planing timbers, and we accepted it, the DIY era and it's wealth of labour saving gadgets had not yet arrived.

Once drilled, the timbers were bolted together, but to give additional strength to the job we would insert timber dogs between the timbers, these were large washers with teeth protruding both sides, which bit into the timbers as the bolts were tightened thus preventing any lateral twist. Now came the task of connecting the two side timbers together, and for this we used nine inch by three inch timbers nailed in position some three feet apart, rather like the rungs of a ladder, and to give added strength to the structure 5/8" diameter rods threaded each end were inserted and drawn up to further hold the two sides together.

At this stage in the construction before the weight became too excessive the whole structure would be raised on sheer legs and block and tackle and dropped on to a metal frame attached to an axle and wheels. This frame which took the form of an inverted A was made from three inch by three inch angle, cut and welded to form the shape with further angle to sit the jetty on, and flat strip cross braces to give lateral strength. This frame some seven feet in height was fitted at the seaward end, the inshore end was essentially a turntable unit as referred to earlier under winter maintenance. The acquisition of suitable axles, wheels and in particular turntables was always a problem, the axles needed to be as light as possible, and relatively plain to allow easy bolting to the A frame. Over the years we had a variety of wheels on the jetties, some of the earlier ones when I arrived on the scene were spoked and did not fare too well in the conditions they were subjected to.

I seem to remember we had axles from Jones Bailing machines and even off one of Rhyl's old "toastracks" as one particular public transport vehicle was affectionately known. For turntables we scoured scrap yards and farms for old carts, some of the wooden chassies were still useable but as long as we could salvage the turntable rings, we could always make a new chassis.

The jetty secured to the A frame and the turntable and wheels set under the inshore end which was only about three feet high; the jetties were raked quite steeply to counteract the natural slope of the beach, the job of decking could be carried out and finally three inch by two inch posts and handrails were fitted.

As I became more and more involved in the construction and maintenance of the jetties, a curious fact stood out. Although the handrail posts were timber, the actual handrails took the form of rope which was threaded through holes in the posts prior to starting a day's work, and always removed at the end of the day because of the fear of vandalism. Apart from the sheer effort this involved, I always felt that ropes, which always had some give in them, were not the ideal safety barrier, and I must confess that it was a rival operator who solved the problem by simply fitting wooden handrails to his jetties. Years of tradition had caused us to overlook the obvious.

The final task on the jetty if it was intended to be the seaward one at which the boat landed was to scrounge old carpet, strips of fire hose and pad the half round timbers we had bolted on the end. If we suffered a rough season the procedure was repeated several times, such was the chafing action of the boat. Thus a jetty was completed and ready for use, the only detail it lacked, and I am sure that this was common to all the landing stages used in Rhyl, and that was brakes. To maintain a braking system in the conditions we worked would have been nigh impossible and yet we cheerfully towed them back and forth along the promenade behind the Bren carriers and winch trucks. I wonder how we would have coped with modern day regulations.

Before closing this chapter I should like to refer again to the acquisition of the Columbian Pine we used for the side members. To obtain timber of those dimensions and quality today would be virtually impossible and the price would be prohibitive, and yet in those days we could walk over the Foryd Bridge to Charles Jone's timber yard and select these long straight planks of knot free golden red timber. There was one occasion I remember when we were obliged to seek further afield for our requirements and I recall travelling to Liverpool with my Uncles to the yard of Seth Bennett a local timber merchant. Here we watched in amazement as the sawyers fed forty foot lengths of twelve inch by four inch through a giant Vee saw, a machine akin to a bandsaw, giving us in a matter of minutes two straight cut and true planks.

THE WORKSHOP

The building that we used as a store and workshop was situated some sixty feet West of Quay Street in the Foryd. Directly on the corner of Quay Street was the Packet Café, a long narrow single storey building with Packet House, a two storey dwelling behind, but connected to the Café. Alongside, to the West of the Café was a piece of ground largely grass, accessed through an ungated opening in a low wall, and then came our workshop.

This was a building some thirty feet deep by twenty feet wide, constructed from a mixture of stone, brick and timber, with a ridged slate roof. I have never been able to ascertain the age of the building, it is clearly visible on photographs of the Robert Jones shipbuilding yard that occupied the triangular site between Quay Street, Wellington Road and the Promenade during the period 1857 to 1878.

Inside the workshop, one corner served to house our fuel supplies, which were contained in a large circular two hundred gallon tank and two forty gallon drums periodically re-filled by tanker vehicles, and we ferried fuel over to the boats in smaller containers. Sharing the same wall would be during the winter months, the buoyancy seats and loose bench seating off the "May Queen", stacked in a very precise manner with the last seat at the top of the pile just clearing the roof eaves.

The opposite side of the workshop would be taken up with piles of Bren Gun carrier tracks, brake drums and sprockets, the end result of our winter visits to scrap dealers in our search for spares, also coils of rope, nets and sundry boat gear. No space was wasted, resting on a beam crossing the building would be the masts and a collection of seventeen-foot long ash oars, a legacy of the Caroline Richardson a sail and pulling RNLI lifeboat. Two of these oars were put into regular use on the 'May Queen' and have got us out of many a tight corner where engines could not be used.

Either side of the door giving access to the rear of the building were our workbenches, on the shorter left hand side was a hand operated grindstone, and our charging area for batteries, on the longer right hand bench we had an engineers vice, and a large, again hand operated drilling machine. Apart from an electric drill and a sander, that was the sum total of our equipment, apart from hand tools, in fact our workshop was without electricity until some time in the fifties when my Uncle decided to have a supply put in.

This was an immense improvement for us, apart from the fact that we could now charge our own batteries and have some heating, it meant that we could put in longer days in winter, the interior of the workshop was always a bit gloomy due to the small windows, and now instead of going home as the daylight faded, or on overcast days, we could work on.

To the rear of the workshop was an open yard area, bounded on the Packet side by a ten foot high stone wall with a gate that led to Packet House, on the South side facing the Marine Lake a similar wall but only about five foot six inches high. The wall to the West side facing the Foryd Bridge always puzzled me, this wall was of brick, again some five and a half feet high with a brick castellated top, but in this wall was a doorway, the door if it ever existed long gone, but the headroom in the doorway was only about four feet. Likewise there was a window opening alongside the doorway some two foot six inches square, but again too low to be useful given the present floor level. Had this been a building at one time with the floor at a much lower level? Outside the wall were concrete bases that may have been part of a three storey building visible on early photographs.

In the yard area we had a stack of pitchpine railway sleepers, on which were stored the portable passenger ramps in winter, there was a stock of steel tubes, angles and flat iron, and a portable blacksmith's forge with hand operated bellows.

Although not used a great deal, there were occasions when we would need to heat a length of angle iron or steel strip to bend or punch holes in, I recall we took the three inch wide metal rim off a very large wheel originally fitted to a water cart, and passing it through the red hot fire foot by foot we straightened it to use for cross braces on a jetty. The coke for the forge came from the local gasworks, which was situated, between Wellington Road and Wood Road, now the Aldi supermarket site, and I used to make the trip for fuel on an old carrier bike that we had at the time.

Also in the yard area was a timber shed which housed a vintage Singer car owned by my Uncle Mr. Stanley Edwards, this car was originally in our workshop but was moved to it's new home to afford us more working space. Alongside this shed stood our tractor.

Outside the yard area we stored the three portable jetties on a piece of land leased from the Rhyl Urban District Council which we fenced off in later years. The remainder of the triangular plot was in the earlier years largely overgrown, Mr Edward Todd lived in Quay Street and his house backed on to the plot as did Sheringdan House owned by Mr. Twigdon. Two wooden telegraph poles stood on the land which we found ideal for 'killing' (taking the stretch out) our cod lines on which we hung our salmon nets. We would spend hours stretching and running our lines around these poles, failure to take the twist out of them would see our nets roll up in the surf.

This triangular area of land was later landscaped by the Council and a pond incorporated in the scheme, as referred to earlier, and today is now a car park with further plans in the pipeline for the future.

I have fond memories of the times spent in the Foryd as I grew up in Rhyl, my Uncle Jack would often allow my brother and I to go to the workshop if he had work to do there, on these occasions my brother would ride on the crossbar of my Uncle's bicycle and I would ride with Mr. Billy Hunt who worked for the family. So would begin a race down the entry from Palace Avenue into Lake Avenue and on towards the Foryd.

In those days the workshop seemed to us to be an Aladdin's cave, full of strange and fascinating objects, there was a drogue used by lifeboats to check their progress in heavy following seas, rat traps, and ferret cages, rabbit snares, a blacksmith's anvil, adzes used by shipbuilders, and a cupboard full of caulking irons, again used by shipwrights to render ships' hulls watertight. In one corner, another cupboard contained medicines and liniments, brushes and a flat metal grooming comb, all associated with the horse that was once used to move the portable jetties. On a peg on the wall would be his bridle and collar.

Perhaps the most interesting item in the workshop was an old trunk of the type often used by seamen, we were told that it belonged to a Captain Wilkes who had sailed to South America and visited Patagonia. He lived in Rhyl in the avenue of that name.

How we wondered what might be in that trunk, our boyish

minds imagined charts relating to buried treasure, or pistols or swords, perhaps even gold coins. We never saw the contents.

Having explored the workshop we would play in the rear yard, at one time my Uncle had obtained some wooden buoyancy boxes from an old lifeboat, and these lay in a huge pile in one corner. We had hours of fun building dens deep in the middle of this collection of boxes of all shapes and sizes. If we behaved ourselves we would occasionally be given a halfpenny or a penny and we would run along the promenade for an ice cream from Mr. Domenico Sidoli who had a cafe in a row of cottages just beyond the Schooner pub but which at that time was called the Foryd Hotel. Mr. Sidoli was the grandfather of Dominic and Maria Sidoli who carry on the family business with their mother in Wellington Road.

Sadly all our childhood landmarks have disappeared, the row of whitewashed cottages and the little outdoor café area were replaced by the Downtown Club and Arcade, the Packet Café and our workshop are now a car park, but at least the memories are still there. Even as I write, plans to further develop this area are being published, hence the need to record the past history of this particular area of Rhyl.

PICTURES

Photo No. 1   Steamer leaving Rhyl Pier circa 1909.

Photo No. 2   Early pleasure boats at Rhyl
Note the steep beach and single loading plank.

A Trip Round The Bay

Photo No. 3   Pleasure boats working off the beach.
Nearest boat the "Majestic"
Photo: estimated 1930's courtesy The County Archivist.

Photo No. 4   Motor Boats working at western end of beach
Note: the wheeled landing plank

PICTURES

Photo No. 5 "Mayflower" working opposite Palace Hotel
Sailing ship with timber delivery in background.

Photo No. 6 "Mayflower" later owned by Mr. Edward Todd.

Photo No. 7   Uncle Charles, Wood Road with horse.

Photo No. 8   T.J. Hughes (Uncle Jack) and crew on "Majestic".

PICTURES

Photo No. 9 "Queen Elizabeth" on Rhyl beach.
Note Horse and single jetty.

Photo No. 10 "Queen Elizabeth" at sea.

Photo No. 11   Launch of "May Queen" at Conwy 1939 from Crossfields' boat yard.

Photo No. 12   "May Queen" as she appeared in the earlier years.

PICTURES

Memorandum

Telephone: CONWAY 3157.

From
JOHN CROSSFIELD & CO.
A. Crossfield - V. Crossfield - I. Crossfield
TIMBER MERCHANTS,
YACHT AND BOAT BUILDERS.
CONWAY,
Motor Boat Installations.   N. WALES.

To

July 31st 1939

The Board of Trade,

Surveyors Office,

Canning Place, LIVERPOOL.

Dear Sirs,

MOTOR PASSENGER LAUNCH 'MAY QUEEN' OF R H Y L.

We are very disappointed at the number of Passengers alloted to this vessel, as when we took the plans to your office in Liverpool we were informed the approximate number this boat would carry would be 130; also when the surveyor Mr.Moore measured her he informed us that the number he had alloted was 120; Mr.Hughes the owner told Mr.Moore that he was disappointed at the number, but he would accept 120. We are writing this letter to you as it is very dissapointing to our client if we are informed that the approximate number that will be carried, then it falls short of the number.

Mr.Hughes was thinking of having another boat built for the next season, but he informes us that after the number he has been alloted for the large boat he does not intend placing another order.

Yours faithfully,
JOHN CROSSFIELD & Co.

SENIOR SHIP SURVEYOR

Photo No. 13   Letter from Crossfield re: seating capacity.

Photo No.14   The "Ocean Queen" original finish, Uncle Stan (on helm) and crew.

Photo No.15   The "Ocean Queen" after re-fit 1952.

PICTURES

Photo No. 16   The "Panther" owned and operated by Robert Gartside approx. 1947

Photo No. 17   The "Wayfarer" owned and operated by Robert Gartside coming into Rhyl for re-fit. 1951

Photo No. 18   The "Wayfarer" after re-fit now named "Royal Princess" 1952

Photo No. 19   The "Duke of Edinburgh" 1949-1958

PICTURES

Photo No. 20 Our Bren Carrier and crew. July 1951

Photo No. 21 T.J. Hughes (Uncle Jack on "May Queen")

Photo No. 22   Keith Staples and Noel Holmes (crew) selecting on board music on "May Queen" Summer of 1951

Photo No. 23   Noel and Glyn (crew) on board "May Queen" 1951

PICTURES

Photo No. 24 The "White Thistle" at High Street.

Photo No. 25 The "White Thistle" laid up for winter.

Photo No. 26   Our workshop (right) and Packet Café Foryd.

Photo No. 27   Our Workshop and jetties Foryd.

PICTURES

Photo No. 28 "May Queen" in Summer season.

Photo No. 29 Passengers disembarking from "May Queen"

Photo No. 30   Timber ship en route to Charles Jones Foryd 1967.

Photo No. 31   "Shearwater" which gave speedboat trips.

Photo No. 32   The Quad, ex. army vehicle with winch which replaced the Bren Gun Carrier.

Photo No. 33   The "May Queen" leaving Rhyl for the last time bound for Fleetwood in April 1967

THE SUMMER SEASON

This was the season that we most looked forward to, after a long winter the thought of getting back on the water and hopefully recouping some of the money we had spent during the winter, was foremost in our minds.

First we had the Board of Trade inspectors to deal with. Just before the "May Queen" came off her winter bed, an inspector from Liverpool would come and inspect the engine that we had dismantled, the buoyancy equipment, fire extinguishers, propeller shafts and the hull. Each inspector had his own particular method of surveying, some would don overalls , boots and a torch and hammer and examine the hull in minute detail whilst we stood by hoping they would not find anything too serious; whether we worked or not that season depended entirely on their findings, other inspectors had a much more casual approach to the inspection, for they knew that it would not be in our interest to cut corners on the maintenance programme, as time out of action in the all too short summer season would cost us dearly.

One inspector in particular springs to mind, he was always concerned over the fact that the nail heads securing the planks to the frames showed rust marks, which bled through the paint. He went to great lengths to tell us how to paint the affected areas with a suitable rustproof primer.

Inspection over we could move the boat off her winter bed, and for the first stage we would allow her to settle on the sloping beach just alongside the sleeper bed, and to prevent her listing over too much we would position a heavily constructed wedge shaped knee under the hull, guided into position by a fore and aft line and a line passed under the keel and secured on the opposite side. The

THE SUMMER SEASON

plan was to move the boat down the sloping beach day by day as the tides dropped, so that eventually we could move to the summer moorings, the other side of the Foryd Bridge, on the first suitable tide.

Once on these moorings which were in the corner of Horton's Nose alongside the stretch of mud and beach to the east of the Quay wall, we could now load up our truck with the buoyancy seats, life-belts, masts etc. trundle round to the Quay, get the boat alongside and off-load.

Easter being a moveable feast, we never expected too much, the tides were usually big, the weather often unsettled; I have seen Easters when we have rowed over to the "May Queen" in a snow fall, but if we did manage to work, it lifted our spirits for the forthcoming season, and of course paid off some of the Winter bills. However before any Easter, we had a second visit from the Board of Trade Inspector, this time for the trials.

The procedure was always the same, the equipment was checked, by this I mean that the life-belts were counted, fire extinguishers identified in their correct positions, the emergency tiller fitted onto the rudder pin on deck, and the rudder swung through it's arc of travel, and finally the trip to sea, where we would be required to carry out such manoeuvres as full turns to port and starboard at speed and going from full ahead to full astern with both engines in order to check our "braking system"

Once satisfied, we would receive the all important Certificate and we were in business. Sea faring folk being superstitious, we would never start the season on a Good Friday, indeed to launch a new boat on a Friday is to be avoided if at all possible, but had we been weak enough to tempt providence, there was never much trade about on that particular day of the holiday. Come Saturday, weather permitting and bright and early before any traffic was on the road, we would start towing the first of the three landing stages, or jetties as we called them, along the promenade and down to the beach via the ramp at the top of Sandringham Avenue.

This was an exceedingly tricky manoeuvre, the slipway entrance was narrow, some 8ft. 6ins. in width, and our widest axle was some 3 or 4 inches less, complicating the problem even more was the toilet wall and embayment wall, halfway down the slipway, creating a corner. To achieve the correct line the driver had to take up a middle of the road position well before the slipway, strike a straight line through the gap, proceed down the slipway until the tractor nearside wheel was almost over the edge, change direction and down onto the sand. If the initial line up was wrong we would shake and bounce the jetty over as best we could, but many a time we grazed the promenade wall, indeed the scars are still visible, one of the few remaining reminders for me of bygone days.

The achievement of a correct line, also had to be made on bringing jetties up from the beach, and I recall one occasion in the season, when the driver missed his line, uncoupled the jetty, immediately lost control of it, and it went over the edge of the slipway, twisting and splitting the side member, rendering the jetty useless. We anxious not to lose any trade, had to form and thread long " U " bolts with associated plates, and splint the damaged side timber, a repair which would have to last the remainder of that season.

Once on the beach, we headed for the seaward end of a wooden groyne opposite Butterton Road, and into one of the softest areas of sand on the Rhyl beach. The four wheel truck could cope on it's own, but not with a fifty two foot jetty in tow, so the procedure was to release the winch wire, drive the truck forward, chock the wheels and winch the jetty up to the truck. This operation was repeated several times until firm ground was reached. In later years we managed to persuade the local Council to remove planks at the promenade end of the groyne, and the problem disappeared.

Depending on the height of the tides, we would set the jetty opposite steps at River Street, or in line with the Coliseum, Will Parkin's open air theatre as it was known then, detach the truck and head back to the workshop for the second jetty. This procedure was repeated until three jetties were set up in line. The seaward one on which the boat would berth was connected to the middle jetty with a short length of chain, but the pulling chain connected to the middle jetty passed under the length of the third, in this way the total weight of the jetties when pulled was not concentrated on one undercarriage, in effect two jetties pushed the third.

In order to keep a straight line when moving, we would sometimes drill a hole in the two turntable rings and drop a bolt in, another method was crude but effective, two flat metal strips with bolts which clamped the two rings together. The question of coupling the jetties together reminds me of the time my Uncle Will who worked on the railway, brought us a carriage coupling to try. The idea was good, shackle the huge links to each axle and turn the bar which wound up the threaded connecter and hey presto the two jetties came together like the 6-45 from Crewe, but the weight of the coupling was too much to cope with, and the idea abandoned.

The work of the beach crew followed a pretty regular pattern. Once set up, the jetties on the incoming tide would be largely out of the water, the seaward end only in water of sufficient depth to allow the boat to make contact. As the tide came in they would be hauled up, the idea being always to allow passengers on and off, something not always possible.

When we worked opposite the Coliseum, the middle section of the beach was very flat, and a gutter used to fill and surround the jetties. If we could time it right and take a half hour trip at this awkward time, the beach crew could pull the jetties up to the final sloping part of the beach. If not, I have seen two forty foot and one fifty foot jetty and three twenty foot portable ramps set out in a single line and passengers negotiating this near two hundred feet walk over the water to get to the boat.

The ebb tide presented a totally different situation, here we would try to push the jetties as far into the water as possible for to be on a beach with a full load of passengers with the tide ebbing, and knowing that you only had inches of water under your keel was very disconcerting. The major problem on the outgoing tide was that the jetty wheels had been standing in soft wet sand for some two to three hours and had settled in. In the days of the bren carriers this was a major problem, sometimes the beach crew would have to dig out the wheels they could get to, in order to relieve the load, but the winch vehicles we used in later years enabled them to first pull the jetties up out of the holes and then charge down the beach with enough impetus to carry them through onto firm ground.

The bren carriers had their limitations, they sat fairly low, were not watertight and we frequently had trouble with water entering the distributor cap which was situated low down on the front of the V8 engine which powered the carrier. I often spent time with the aid of a mirror, for such was the inaccessible position of the distributor, cleaning and adjusting the contact breaker points. On several occasions we would return from a trip, dismayed to see that the jetties had not been pulled up, and the Bren carrier partly submerged and the beach crew frantically trying to start the engine.

Although there was keen and often hostile rivalry among the pleasure boat operators, there was an unwritten rule that in dire emergencies we would help each other, and hauling the other operators stalled tractor out was such an emergency, as not one of us could guarantee that we would not be in that situation at some time.

One novel but disastrous idea that came up at the time, to try and save immersing the bren carrier when pushing the jetties down, was to bury a weight or anchor at the seaward end of the line to which was attached a jenny wheel, as used by builders to haul buckets etc. up to a roof site. A rope was attached to the second jetty, passed round the wheel and led up the beach, the idea being to drive up the beach and draw the jetties down rather like a roller blind, but despite all our efforts we kept dragging the buried wheel out of the sand and up the beach.

The jetties when not in use, would except for exceptionally high tides be kept on the beach, if working by the Coliseum one of the three would be taken off and turned parallel to the promenade wall. If bad weather threatened all three would be taken to a relatively high part of the beach at the top of River Street. Rhyl in those days was so busy during the peak Summer months that any major moving of jetties had to be carried out when the beach visitors had gone home or back to their respective boarding houses. We did try whenever possible not to disturb holiday-makers too much, some were very understanding, others would refuse to budge once they had set their deck chairs up, and very often the beach crew would have to leave the carrier or truck on the beach until evening, so dense were the crowds. How different the picture is today, and at the time this inconvenience bothered us, but looking back one realizes that Bren carriers and four-wheel trucks don't mix with visitors and young children.

Whilst on this theme, some bright spark on the local council decided that the jetties looked unsightly on the beach and should be removed daily. Mr. Edward Todd who worked the High Street pitch decided to oblige the councillor and proceeded to remove all the jetties via the High Street slipway and the busy promenade, all the way to the Foryd and return the next day. The result was that massive traffic jams built up and the idea was scrapped within days. However leaving the jetties on the beach was not without it's problems, they were an obvious playground for children, indeed many was the time as a child I had clambered onto the structures, run along the decking and jumped off the end, and made swings from the ropes which they used to leave on in those days, but we often found that the tyres had been let down or the valves smashed with stones, and occasionally attempts would be made to push them into the sea. I shudder to think what would have happened to them in this day and age.

Once Easter was over, we had six or seven weeks before the Whitsun break, and this was the period when we took advantage of the longer days and warmer weather to spruce up the boat or boats.

In the days of the earlier passenger boats and indeed up to the 1950's the hulls were varnished, it was only when Robert Gartside brought the "Duke of Edinburgh" to Rhyl in 1949 resplendent in white paint that ourselves and the other operator Edward Todd realized that we had to move with the times. Our first task would be to chip and de-rust any metalwork, mainly the railings behind the outside seats and re-paint silver. Then would come the fixed slatted seats around the deck perimeter, some one hundred and twenty feet of them, scraped and sanded and re-varnished. Even those finished up being painted in the final years.

The big task was the hull, and to carry out this work we would put the "May Queen" on a sandbank in the Harbour where she would dry out for long periods. The hull would be thoroughly sanded, the red waterline section masked off and a coat of International undercoat applied followed by a coat of yacht enamel. Even as we endeavoured to get a professional mirror like finish, we knew that come the first rough day the seams in the hull planks would compress as the hull flexed, squeezing the putty in the seams out ever so slightly and spoiling our finish.

My late Uncle had an idea he had picked up from a fairground operator, which was to give the final gloss coat a thin coat of clear varnish. This we did one season, struggling to see where we had applied it as we went, and then finding that by the end of the season it had flaked in places. Needless to say, we had a mammoth task the following year having had to sand all the old varnish off before re-painting. Every year Edward Todd would have us guessing as to his chosen colour for the season, we would suddenly see the "White Thistle" in a pale cream colour and think how nice she looked and perhaps wondered whether we should consider a change of colour. Next minute she would be back in white and we realized that he was using a slightly different coloured undercoat to make the application of the white gloss more easily seen.

The main hull finished we would repeat the procedure on the waterline, an area which was very critical to a boat's appearance. The lowering or raising of the waterline colour could increase or reduce very effectively the freeboard appearance, ie. height above the water. The underwater areas of the hull had already been painted whilst the boat was on the winter bed and reasonably accessible, alas not with an anti-fouling, but with a black bitumen paint which would give us performance problems later in the season, as referred to in my chapter on the winter programme. With any luck and given good weather, by Whitsun the "May Queen" and indeed all the passenger boats would be looking their best and we would be longing for a change of routine although we were well aware that we were facing three or four months of very irregular work patterns.

A typical working day would see us arrive at the workshop, the beach crew would set off to prepare the jetties, and we would fill two five gallon tins with diesel fuel, and row across to the boat. Here we would check oil and water levels on the engines, inspect the sea cock filters, a very important chore, working the beach as we did, meant that we picked up jellyfish and passing debris very often, and a clogged filter soon led to overheating. Whilst this was being done, a crew member would run up the flags and set the colourful bunting which ran down the mast stays and the back stay to the funnel. As soon as the flood tide reached a certain mark we would let go fore and aft moorings swing out into the river and proceed round to the beach.

In the earlier days of boating at Rhyl, the procedure for holding the boat whilst at the jetty would have been the use of a long pole, the operator standing in the stern and holding the boat square on to the jetty to counteract the effect of the tide flowing along the beach. As boats got bigger this pole was replaced with an anchor and rope, and for several years I was anchor man. As we got near the jetty and at a signal from the skipper I would let go the stern anchor, a large fisherman's pattern, and pay out rope until we touched the jetty. On the incoming tide we would keep the anchor rope as short as possible knowing that soon the jetties would require pulling up, and consequently anchor rope would have to be paid out, and too much rope out meant a long slow haul back to the anchor when we left for our trip. On the ebb tide the reverse took place, a long length of anchor rope would be paid out, if we thought the jetties would be pushed down whilst we were there.

As well as having to take all the above into account, there was the added problem of wind and tide. The dominant tide flow along the beach was East to West, and we allowed for this when lining up for the jetty, the stronger the flow the more we kept up tide, the wind played a big factor where the "May Queen" was involved, so shallow was her draught which gave her a tendency to drift very easily. A strong South Westerly wind would mean approaching the jetty some forty or fifty yards up wind, dropping the anchor and literally motoring in and drifting down , at the same time checking with the anchor at the right moment which would send the bow crashing against the jetty to the point where one outer wheel would momentarily lift up and drop back.

It required a lot of practice to effect perfect dockings at the jetty, and when I was allowed to try my hand under the watchful eye of my uncle, I often got it wrong, much to the annoyance of the anchor man, who would have to haul the anchor in as we backed out to start the run in again. I mentioned the fisherman's anchor that we used, a pattern recognised by most people, two flukes and a folding stock, weighing some 40 to 45 pounds, attached to a coil of four and a half inch circumference hemp rope.

The anchor itself was heavy enough to lift, but when a twenty ton boat had been pulling on it for some twenty minutes it had really dug itself into the sand and to physically haul it out leaning over the stern rail was very hard work, in fact at some stage I pulled a disc in my spine which troubled me for some years. We also went on to try a "danforth" anchor which was more of a plough shape, much lighter but very much more effective which made my job even more arduous. There was also the time that we tried using coir rope, very much easier to handle, but the problem was that it floated on the surface and stretched when tension was applied making it most unsuitable for holding a boat steady at a jetty. How I looked forward to those windless days when we could use the small light fisherman's anchor which we carried.

All the above factors, strength of tides, direction of wind, sea conditions on the flood and the ebb, size of anchors to use, all had to be considered, on some days each trip could present a different set of problems, and we were very much in tune with the elements, even today some forty years on, I tend to watch the cloud movements and note changes in wind direction, in the same way that farmers are at one with the elements.

I mentioned earlier the irregular work pattern we experienced, in actual fact there was also a certain regularity to it, for as we followed the tide tables we would repeat our work rota every two weeks. If high water was at 9am.we could manage one trip off the main beach and disembark passengers in the river opposite Sydenham Avenue. Landing facilities were very limited at the time, the pier was impossible, the Quay was in private hands, although we occasionally used it in emergencies, but the tide rips and small craft in the Harbour made this manoeuvre difficult, in later years a new slipway would be built at Sydenham Avenue, too far ahead in time to be of any benefit to us

. When we could only manage one morning trip we would then moor the "May Queen" in the river and work the next incoming evening tide until dark. As the tides moved on through the day we followed them and soon we worked full mornings and then afternoons and the evening tides finished. When the tides were very small we would move the boat to "bottom ferry" this being the local name for the stretch of the River Clwyd opposite Sydenham Avenue, and by so doing we could steal a trip before the flood tide reached the Harbour

We would drop out of the Harbour on the last of the ebb tide usually between six and seven in the morning, put the bow lightly ashore on the river bank, swing round, run our stern anchor and rope to the bow and moor up. We would then run a bow line to the training wall which on the flood tide would be transferred to the stern to prevent the boat from swinging round too early.

As I write this I recall a time when some of the pleasure boats, would on very small tides, again drop out of the Harbour on the last of the ebb tide, but instead of mooring at bottom ferry, they would continue down to a gravel bank between the third and fourth perch on the training wall, and moor up there to await the flood tide.

Why they did this I am not sure, but two possible explanations spring to mind, one, they may have been considering the local ferry men who worked bottom ferry, leaving them a clear river on which to ply their trade, and two, having gone so far down river, the obvious first trip was going to be off the main beach, and they would follow the flood tide up the beach and turn into a gutter opposite John Street, into which the jetties would have been pushed down.

How I loved those early summer mornings, it was so peaceful, the occasional early visitor would be out before breakfast, sometimes a salmon would turn in the river, and on some mornings the local netsmen would gather to start their leisurely turns down the "run" with their nets to catch salmon and sea trout. When the fish were really running in large numbers, usually around the third week in June, we would join them, sometimes just to take our turn in the river and very often staying out for the tide. This made for a very long day for as soon as there was water up the river, we would stop fishing and return to trips around the bay, and still hopefully have fish to sell that day; our leisurely days in the winter soon gave way to very long and arduous summer days; indeed, I was looking through some old Rhyl Guides recently, and was able to recall the names of the guest houses and those of my customers, who bought salmon off us during the Summer season. Some of the visitors to Rhyl, ate very well when fresh salmon was on the menu.

Perhaps this is the time to explain what sort of service we were able to provide to the thousands of visitors who came to Rhyl every summer. Whenever the tide was in and the weather settled we could operate off the main beach for a maximum of five hours a day on tides up to twenty eight feet (8.5m.) and we would work opposite the Coliseum which gave us approximately two and a half hours either side of high water. Tides above that height would see us opposite River Street on two jetties, our time cut to three and a half to four hours due to a large bank outside us.

We provided half hour cruises most of which we made along the coast towards Abergele, our turning point being marked by lining up a whitewashed cottage inland by St. George's quarry and Towyn church. We operated under a Steam 6 Certificate which allowed us short sea voyages no longer than three miles from the point of embarkation, and within one and a half miles of the coast. There was also a Steam 5 Certificate which applied to vessels operating in rivers, and usually permitted more passengers to be carried. The "May Queen" could carry 115 passengers in great comfort, and being decked afforded good views for all on board. Once we had left the beach and checked temperature and oil gauges, looked over the side to make sure that there was that all important flow of cooling water from the pumps, which always prompted the question usually in a midlands accent, "are we sinking skip?" we would start collecting fares. In those days it was two shillings and sixpence (twelve and a half pence today) for adults and one shilling (five pence) for children.

Whilst we did this the passengers would be entertained by Mr. Tony Ward and his accordion who was a popular and well-known figure on the boat for many years. When he left us we fitted loud speakers to the mast and touted for trade through a microphone and played gramophone records. Artists popular with the passengers were Guy Mitchell and Mario Lanza, and the words and music of "Pretty Little Black Eyed Susie" "My Truly Truly Fair" and " Be My Love "often rang out across the beach.

Music on the boats was nothing new, I have referred earlier in my book to my recollections of a young boy violinist and a harpist on the "Queen Elizabeth" the predecessor to the "May Queen", Robert Gartside also had a lady accordionist on the "Duke of Edinburgh", who I was informed recently was named Amy Humphries, and I hope that I have used the correct spelling for her name.

As I mentioned earlier, most of our trips started and finished on the main beach, but occasionally the timing of our last trip would mean that we would not be able to return to the beach, which meant we would have to disembark our passengers on the river bank opposite Sydenham Avenue. For this contingency we in later years kept a twenty foot ramp chained to the sloping apron on the seaward side of the promenade wall, and the metal fastening lugs are still there to this day. Previous to this practice we would sling a ramp off the beach stock across the bow and take it with us on the trip.

A Trip Round The Bay

I was never too happy about finishing a trip at this point in the river, especially on big tides, the main flow of the ebb came downstream but the concrete chamber housing the sewer outlet created a strong eddy, and to add to this problem two small storm drain pipes protruded out of the bank where we had to land. As you turned across the tide, the eddy tide would grip the bow area and swing you towards these pipes which were still submerged just below the surface, and you could only hope that you had judged your approach correctly, and that the bow would strike the beach where predicted.

Some times if we arrived at this point when the day-trippers were pouring onto the beach from the coach park we could sneak in an extra trip. This again had it's problems, the beach shelved very slowly at this particular part of the tide, which meant that we had very little water under a considerable length of the keel, and driving ahead on one engine to hold the boat on the bank meant that we started to dry out very quickly, plus the fact that we were loading passengers who all wanted to sit near the front.

On many occasions I thought that I had left it too late to pull the boat off, so quickly did the tide ebb, the only remedy was to ask the passengers to move to the stern, with the promise that they could return to the bow after, and put both engines full astern until we floated again. This procedure was often necessary several times in the course of loading.

When it was time for the trip the eddy tide was our friend, with the aid of an ex-lifeboat 17 foot oar, the crew member would push the bow out into the fast flowing ebb, the eddy would grip the stern, and I would hold the boat on the engines while the opposite forces of the tide swung us like a top, gauging the exact moment to go full ahead before we crabbed sideways onto the training wall.

In describing the above procedure I would come to envy Robert Gartside's "Duke of Edinburgh", the boat he was to purchase later. She had the advantage of post war technology in the form of twin rudders. This meant that unlike a single rudder which was in relatively dead water when not moving ahead, twin rudders were in direct line with the propellers and acted on the flow from them, with the result that the power from both engines could be used. The result was that the "Duke" could slew round against the ebb until square on to the beach, pull off and exit the river very easily.

When in my foreword I mentioned the period 1936-1967, I must clarify this statement a little. True I remember as a young boy the "Majestic", "Duchess of York" and others, but my working life on the boats started in 1947 as I explained in the first part of the Winter programme chapter. At that time there was the "May Queen" owned by my uncle, there was also the "Pirate "a 26 foot converted cabin cruiser carrying 28 passengers which was the first boat to be owned by Robert Gartside, and had come on the boating scene in 1946, and at that time Phil Jones worked with him. Robert Gartside had been in the catering trade at the Westbourne Café by the Marine Lake, and decided that he would join the motorboat industry, seeing the potential rise in trade, now that the war was over. He established a yard and covered accommodation for what would become several boats, on the river bank alongside the railway down Green Avenue, and traded as Rhyl Marine Trading Co. Ltd.

In 1947 the year I started, the effects of the training wall completed in 1937 were making themselves known on the main beach, material from the west which normally would have been carried by successive tides and find it's way on to the beach and maintaining a steady slope, was now being swept past the end perch and down the east and up the River Dee. The result was that we were working a beach that was getting progressively flatter, and we were forced to use two and sometimes three jetties, but trade was good and that encouraged us to keep going.

In 1947 Robert Gartside purchased another boat the "Panther "an ex-government 36 foot harbour launch, and after modifications he put her into service for that season, and she was skippered by Phil Jones, and Robert ran the "Pirate", but it was becoming clear that the public preferred the decked boat, and in 1949 he brought the "Duke of Edinburgh," built by Johnson and Jago of Leigh on Sea, to Rhyl. She was some fifty feet in length with fifteen foot beam, and again as with all the passenger boats working the Rhyl beach, she was of shallow draught.

By this time, Edward Todd who had been in the passenger boat business before the war, was anxious to get back into the trade, and in 1948 he worked the "White Thistle "a larger vessel than the "White Thistle" IV with Phil Jones, who by this time had joined him.

As I recall, we all enjoyed a reasonable working relationship, we would work between River Street and John Street, as did Robert Gartside, and Teddy Todd, as we knew him, would work opposite High Street. Trade was good, the war was over, and holidays were back on the agenda. Even the weather seemed better in those days, although the diary I kept, often testified to long spells of windy and unsettled weather.

When the "Duke of Edinburgh" arrived in Rhyl, the speculation among the local boatmen, and I must admit that I too fell for the theory, having been used to cruiser sterns, that the "Duke" would not be suitable for the job, she had a high straight stem and a square stern. "She will be up the beach in no time if a sea hits that stern" was the general comment. In actual fact the "square" stern upon inspection revealed that it had a curve to it, and a clever uplift to the hull at the water line meant that waves broke under the stern rather than on it.

As I previously mentioned, Robert Gartside's new boat, had some very good features she was lighter than the "May Queen" being built of larch on oak frames, a good sea boat, twin screw, with two rudders, which made her very manoeuvrable in all conditions, our boat with the single rudder required a very large turning circle in windy conditions, but she was strong and despite being built in 1939 she is still in service to this day.

In 1951, no doubt encouraged by the success of the "Duke" Robert brought to Rhyl a boat at that time called the "Wayfarer" which was built in the United States as a high speed commuter, and sold off by Small Craft Disposals. Our response to this was for Uncle Jack and Uncle Stan to commission David Williams and Sons of Aberystwyth to build us a new boat. She was an open boat forty seven feet long and a beam of thirteen foot six inches by two foot draught, mahogany planks on oak frames, and licensed to carry ninety six passengers. We named her "Ocean Queen "and she was skippered for a time by Mr. Will Hughes who had retired from the railway, but it was my Uncle Stan who became responsible for her for the greater part of the time she was at Rhyl.

The arrival of the "Ocean Queen" meant that we needed more jetties, so that she could operate separately, and this was duly done, a second carrier was purchased, and boat and beach crew recruited. At one time we employed some six persons.

During the winter of 1951, Robert Gartside completely gutted the "Wayfarer", the topsides were raised and she was decked, and two diesel engines installed, and she was now capable of carrying eighty four passengers. In this work Robert was assisted greatly by Fred Rastin who worked with him and was a very skilful joiner and good all round tradesman, and it was Fred who skippered the "Wayfarer" now named "Royal Princess" for the 1952 season.

We too had been busy, the "Ocean Queen " when built had a varnished hull and a small bridge aft and engine box. Uncle Stan and I proceeded to move the bridge to a more forward position and fitted a dummy funnel on the engine box, and the hull was painted white. It was all about image, there was something attractive about a gleaming white hull, compared to a rather drab varnish finish which tended to weather very quickly, and funnels were definitely in fashion at the time, and of course the children, among our passengers were always looking for what they considered to be the "fastest" boat.

Now the "May Queen" had never really been fast, she was originally fitted from new with two 28hp. Lister diesels, and in my opinion underpowered, as seemed to be the problem with many boats at that time, so lacking in power was she that I have seen the time when returning to Harbour on a big ebb tide, we would be brought to a standstill, unable to stem the tide, and having to resort to holding the boat off the bank in the narrows with long oars, until the tide slackened.

In 1952 my Uncle Jack decided that the "May Queen" needed a bit of a makeover, and we took her to Dickies of Bangor. Here an additional strake was fitted above the deck line, which had the effect of increasing her freeboard, ie. that part of the hull above the water. The old engines were taken out and two 48hp. Lister Freedom range engines were fitted, these were a new type of medium/ high speed engine, fresh water cooled, and when the installation was complete, the engine room was a maze of copper pipes, heat exchangers and water tanks.

Thus was the scene on Rhyl beach in the early 1950's, there was the "May Queen" capable of carrying 115 passengers, the "Duke of Edinburgh" 86 passengers, the "Ocean Queen" 96, the "Royal Princess"84 and the "White Thistle" nearly 100 passengers.

Such was the holiday season in Rhyl at that time, that I have seen all five boats waiting at their respective jetties, on a perfect summer morning, ready for when the visitors would pour out of the many guest houses between Palace Avenue and Abbey Street, onto the promenade almost as if from a given signal. Some would choose to hire a deckchair, others to stroll along the prom, but I have seen all five pleasure boats leaving the beach just after 10am. All full or certainly almost full.

During the peak of the season, Teddy Todd would put the "Mayflower" into commission, which although having a small passenger carrying capacity, would nevertheless take the surplus of the visitors left by the "Thistle," thus preventing them straying down to the other boats. When there were long queues for the boats and we had to turn visitors away and hope that they would wait for the next trip, there was the temptation to overload, the "May Queen" although licensed to carry 115 persons could accommodate 150, the seating area per person was calculated by the Board of Trade, and there was always the possibility that one of their inspectors could be on the promenade, checking numbers. We were obliged to stick to the regulations, to disregard them could have lost any one of us our licence.

The reader will have realized by now that competition

between the boat operators was pretty fierce, we I suppose felt annoyed that our system of operating boats and jetties, perfected after years of trial and error, should be so easily emulated by others. Edward Todd was the only pleasure boat at the High Street pitch and he was spared the main cut and thrust of the competition. The other side of the coin was that the competition improved trade, in as much that it focussed the public eye on the beach. They enjoyed the competitive touting, the musicians on the boats trying to outplay each other, and of course there was always the added thrill of seeing a bren carrier throw it's tracks, or fail to start on the incoming tide. It is also true to say that the boats that came to Rhyl were smart vessels, with white painted hulls and topsides and be-decked with colourful bunting. I think that by then we had all come to realize that showmanship played a big part in the equation.

It is fair to say that we were very limited by weather conditions, working as we were off a very flat beach, and even if we were able to pick up passengers at the beach we had to take into account the conditions at sea, a strong south westerly could when blowing against the ebb tide produce a lively sea, the river ebbing on a big tide into an opposing wind could produce a nasty fall-out. I recall one occasion in such conditions, meeting a stray salmon net stretching across the full width of the river and barely visible in the troughs, and despite going full astern on both engines, the net continued to slide under the hull, just stopping short of the propellers as we gained astern momentum. To have been without propellers with a boat full of passengers on the ebb tide did not bear thinking about at the time.

This brings me to the question of safety, despite the fact that over the years between all the boats we must have carried many thousands of visitors in all sorts of conditions, precarious walks over water on planks, shaking jetties and heaving decks, and even at dusk with torches when we were lucky enough to pull a crowd from Will Parkin when he closed at 9pm., and yet we had a remarkable safety record. We always had a rule that the bow of the boat and the seaward end of the jetty were never left unattended, but I can recall just one incident on our boat when a blind lady, whose companion failed to tell us of her condition, fell between the boat and the jetty. Fortunately she was unharmed but obviously distressed.

Coupled with this safety record was the fact that all the boats at some time were responsible for saving lives, swimmers in difficulty, children and inflatables blown out to sea, all can thank the passenger boats and their crews for being on the scene at the time. Another thing we were good at was recovering beach balls, for every time there was an offshore wind, dozens of balls would be blown out to sea. We constructed a long handled net and by the end of the season we had a fair stock of balls of all sizes and colour. Very often the owner of a lost ball would see us recover it and be awaiting our return in order to reclaim it, but even so we were able to take a good number to a childrens' home in Brighton Road.

The halcyon days of summer passed all too quickly, in early June we had the season ahead of us, the schools broke up in July and before we knew it the shorter days of September were upon us and another season had passed by.

Each day was different, the weather in all it's moods gave us calm days, the boat gently nudging the jetty, other days were windy, rough seas and all of us stretched to the limit coping with conditions. Every Summer we would get the occasional day when we encountered sea fog. We would keep working for it could clear as quickly as it came, but in order to continue with our trips we would bring from below, a large compass and position it on deck away from any metal objects. We would then set a course straight out from the beach and return on a reciprocal course, hoping that the corrections that we had made to take into account the tide run which would be on our beam either from the West or East depending on the time of high water, had not carried us too far from our landing point. In conditions like this it was very easy to become disorientated and imagine that you were going in the wrong direction, and the temptation to ignore the compass reading was very strong. Another strange effect in fog is that it is very difficult to distinguish which direction sounds are coming from. We also met, albeit for a very short time, interesting people, who would come up to the bridge and ask questions about the area and how we operated. I always found plenty to do, the engines needed constant checking for oil pressures and water temperatures and I kept a daily log of these, hours run each day and weather conditions.

I recall one summer when our workload was increased through an idea which I believe was sold to my Uncle by some one from Snow Goose Ices who had a depot in Ffordd Las. The plan was to put a cold cabinet on the "May Queen" filled with ice for the day, because we had no mains supply on board, from which we would sell ices to the passengers. They, Snow Goose would bring us a supply to the beach as we started work, and in theory take unsold items back at the end of the tide. This was fine as long as we worked a full tide, but if adverse weather conditions forced an early finish, no-one called to collect the stock, and we were left with rapidly melting goods. Coupled with the fact that selling ices made demands on an already busy crew, the idea was soon shelved.

Now a word about the boat and beach crew characters who

worked for us. When we operated two boats, we employed some six men, who came from all walks of life, several were college students working during their vacations, one crew member lived with his family at a butchers shop in Grange Road, and whenever he was late for work would offer me a meat coupon. Another was a Wimbledon fan, and felt that tennis was more important than work during that fortnight. Needless to say he was soon able to watch as much tennis as he liked.

Our most enthusiastic member was a young boy whose duty that day was to throw an anchor over the bow at a given signal from me. He became so intent on watching me, that he resembled a sprung trap, and when the order "now" came he jumped overboard with the anchor, and falling under the bows as he did, I feared the worst, but upon hauling in the rope, we were all relieved to see him still clinging to the anchor.

Perhaps the most colourful character was an Australian called Bob Crawford, who lived during the summer in a caravan on the Warren at Talacre. He used to turn up for work with a parcel of blood stained newspaper, in which was a bullock's heart, and proceed to store it on the boat for that tide.. I tried him on the stern as anchorman for a time, but when instructed to throw the anchor, he first had a habit of giving me the thumbs up sign, followed by "gotcha mate" or "righto" in his broad Aussie accent, during which time the boat was rapidly approaching the jetty. We soon found him other duties. There is no doubt that our most loyal and youngest helper was Roger Hardwick. Roger lived in Abbey Street with his mother who had a shop, and when he was not helping in the shop, and not in school, he spent most of his time on the beach with us, helping on the boat and on the beach. I recall one night when an unusually high tide was threatening to float our jetties out to sea, I had gone up to the prom, and was in the water trying to hold the jetties, when I heard a splash in the darkness and there was Roger like a seal swimming alongside me. Between us we managed to hold the jetties until the tide receded and they were safe.

Other names that spring to mind, are Keith Staples, Ken Rowlands, Peter Fairclough, Bernie Evans and Noel Holmes. There was also a young boy named Fred Johnson, who came from the Stoke-on-Trent area. Every year, young Fred would come to Rhyl with his parents, book in at the "Water's Edge" guest house in Rhyl, and come looking for us, and spend much of his holiday on the boat, helping out when required. Sadly Fred passed away in 2009. Another good friend of mine Mr. Cecil Biddulph gained his sea legs on the "May Queen" all those years ago, which no doubt prepared him for the cruises he now takes in later life.

Those of my old crew, who are left, are mostly scattered far and wide, but they always keep in touch, and when we meet we reminisce about what they describe as the best years in their lives.

Apart from those of our crew, the passenger boat industry created many jobs for the local fishermen and boatmen in the harbour. I remember Mr. Harold Campini and Mr. Marcel Vogelsberger, working for Bob Gartside, and the late Mr. Jackie Alcock and Mr. Ian Armstrong were also involved. Coming as I do from a large seafaring family, my Grandfather Joseph Hughes was coxswain of the Rhyl lifeboat Caroline Richardson, on which my Uncle Jack had been a crew member, several of my relatives also worked on our pleasure boats. This was the unique and wonderful academy of learning that the Foryd could offer; there was always a group of youngsters, who crewed on the boats, learnt to row and scull, how to splice ropes, skills which would stay with them into their adult lives, and indeed many went on to take up sea-faring activities.

The fact that we had a considerable staff presented us with problems on days when it was too rough to work. The main tasks had of course been carried out before the season started, so it was a case of finding little maintenance jobs for them to do. When we had the bren carriers there would be brake linkages to free off, tracks shortened and tightened, wheel hubs greased, and when we changed to 4x4 trucks the winch wire always needed running out for cleaning and greasing. The jetties sometimes needed attention, perhaps a deck plank had to be replaced or re-fixed, and life was much easier for the beach crews if the turntable rings were cleaned and greased.

On the days when we decided to go fishing for salmon, we would dismiss them almost as soon as they arrived, they did in fact have quite a good life for the relatively short time they were employed by us, admittedly they were on call seven days a week, but their working day was no more than six hours, and very often less such was the weather in an average summer, and they had many days off on pay, for we paid them a weekly wage.

One period of very bad weather always stays in my mind, we had three weeks of west to north west winds and not a boat made a single trip, and within the first week we had used up all the odd maintenance jobs, and we could sense that the crews were fed up with the inactivity, so we split them into two groups. We had in our yard a stack of old railway sleepers, which the one group cut into sections and converted them into firewood, and needless to say my Uncle Stan and myself had kindling for our fires all through the following winter. The second group were given tins of Brasso and polishing cloths and put aboard the "May Queen" to work in the engine room, where a great number of copper pipes had been introduced as a result of the new engine installation in 1952. These, the lads proceeded to burnish, they painted the walls and ceiling and even the boards in the walkways, until the engine room would have done credit to a museum. Needless to say that once we started passenger work again I am afraid that the pipes soon became tarnished again.

During the summer seasons we would occasionally receive notice that a timber ship was due to berth at Rhyl to deliver timber to Charles Jone's yard on the quay. These vessels came from Norway and Sweden and despite their size they were relatively shallow draughted. They would creep in on dead high water, usually piloted by Phil Jones, and we, because we were moored in the corner by the Quay, would be on board with engines running and moorings ready for quick release. This procedure was particularly important when the vessel was leaving, she would turn and move away from the Quay by means of a spring rope, cross a middle sandbank and exit the harbour, if this manoeuvre had gone wrong, she would have drifted down onto us.

The one thing that our crew members all through the years had in common was their love of the job. They had fresh air, sunshine, a steady wage and for the younger ones, the chance to chat up the young ladies on the boat and on the beach. I still keep in touch with Noel Holmes, who spent several seasons with us, and he always maintains to this day that they were the happiest days in his life.

For the latter part of the 1940's and the early part of the 1950's the passenger boat industry enjoyed good times, but subtle changes were taking place.

The beach as mentioned earlier was increasingly being influenced by the construction of the River Training Wall and was becoming flat with very little safe high ground near the promenade wall. This meant that our jetties needed to be longer, more portable ramps were needed to span gullies, all putting an increased burden on beach crews and our vehicles, also the public attitude to holidays was changing, destinations abroad were becoming more enticing, and around Rhyl, caravan parks were becoming popular, these with the on site facilities such as shops and bars were bringing about a change in peoples habits. Gone to some extent was the early turnout that we had come to expect, and an early departure for the camps in the late afternoon affected our evening tides, as very few returned to savour what was to my mind the loveliest time of the day for a sail. The heat of the day had gone, very often the breeze would die away, and we witnessed some spectacular sunsets.

I suppose 1954 was the signal to us that the best years had gone when Robert Gartside decided to sell the "Royal Princess." She was sold to I believe to a well known industrialist, converted into a motor yacht and cruised the east coast of Ireland. I am indebted to Mr. D.W. Harris, whose book the Maritime History of Rhyl and Rhuddlan reminded me of the event. The exact year escapes me but before 1955 we were approached by an oil company who were looking for a tender to operate at Qatar in the Persian Gulf, and no doubt influenced by the earlier departure of the "Princess", we decided to sell the "Ocean Queen," the boat in which they had expressed an interest.

My Uncle Stan and myself had the very enjoyable task of taking her by sea up the River Dee, along the Shropshire Union canal which runs through the heart of Chester and into the Manchester Ship Canal at Eastham Locks, and on to Manchester Docks. Two events from that journey stay in my mind, the first was that on entering the Chester lock, we had literally one inch to spare either side of the boat, in fact I remember some players from Chester Football Club, out training, swinging on the lock gate arms to crush the rubbish that had built up between the gates and the wall, thus just allowing us to squeeze through.

The second memory is that of arriving at Manchester Docks and having to scale for the first time in my life, a rope ladder to enable us to get aboard the freighter which was to transport our boat to the Gulf. The long swaying ladder, the arm aching climb up the towering side of the ship, and looking down at the "Ocean Queen" dwarfed by the surroundings, is something I can easily recall.

We were then basically back to the situation where the passenger boats were left to work a deteriorating beach, and fewer passengers. In 1958 Robert Gartside suddenly appeared at our workshop and announced that he was selling the "Duke of Edinburgh," and that she would be working on the Thames by Westminster Pier. We were somewhat surprised, but my Uncle Jack who had passed away in 1957, had always expressed the wish that we should carry on as long as possible, so we, along with Edward Todd were now the remaining two large passenger boats. It was about this time that we became a limited company on the advice of our accountants, and we had a sign on our workshop door and a shiny brass plate proudly saying L and E Marine Ltd. on the wall at our accountant's office in Kinmel Street. The L was my surname, and the E was Edwards, my Uncle Stan's surname, and my wife designed cap badges for us, using the two initials.

One would expect that with two boats less on the scene, our trade would have increased dramatically, but it was not the case. The competitive spirit which the public seemed to enjoy had disappeared, and whilst trade was reasonable, the whole pace had become much slower. We had also noticed a slight change in the publics' approach to their leisure activities, whereas in previous years they seemed perfectly happy to sit on the boat, listening to the music for up to twenty minutes before we cast off for the trip, now we were being asked more and more how much longer they would have to wait. The trend particularly among the younger generation was for speed, even at the expense of shorter rides.

Anxious to move with the times, we purchased from Windboats of Wroxham on the Norfolk Broads, a Pearly Monarch aluminium hull, powered by a Volvo- Penta inboard/outboard drive, and capable of twenty to twenty five knots. This boat skippered by my Uncle Stan, worked mainly from the corner of the River at Sydenham Avenue, but upon approaching the Council, we received permission to operate at times from the main beach. To enable us to do this, using scaffold pipes and clips, we formed a sloping ramp at one side of the seaward end of our main jetty, taking care to design it so that it was still within our wheelbase width, and could negotiate the access ramp to the beach. Thus we were able to cater for all sectors of the public, and we soldiered on through the early part of the sixties, making a reasonable living from the business.

By this time several fast boats had appeared on the scene, the first was Ray Rodgers, who in 1959 ran speedboat trips in his Fletcher 007, followed by Peter Bennison, then Peter Campini, Billie Hunt, Iowerth Thomas, Tommy Lancaster and Harry Smith. These all operated from the River opposite Sydenham Avenue.

As I mentioned earlier, we were directly responsible to the Board of Trade for our licence to operate the big boats, but the local council issued licences for the smaller boats. This was because they owned the "right of way" across the foreshore, the stretch of beach which was used by our customers to get to the boats, and they were able to levy a charge on us and issue licences to operate. An official from the council, once approached us on the beach, on a day when we were particularly stressed, to inform us that the council were considering charging us for the use of the beach by the big boats. I don't think he realized what an asset to the town we were, and he was sent on his way with a flea in his ear, and we heard nothing more about the matter. However we had to concede to the charges for the smaller boats, and every year we would attend the licensing meeting at the Council Offices in Prestatyn, along with the beach donkey proprietors, and the hackney cab drivers, and hope that the powers that be would renew our licence. Once we found that we could operate, our boat and equipment was checked by the council appointed Boating Inspector, to whom we were answerable, and who was able to dictate the conditions we could operate in. Over the years there were many Inspectors, and the names that spring to mind are, Edward Todd, Harry Hughes and Jack Connell, and again, as with the bigger boats, we all had a very good safety record.

I mentioned earlier that we were making a reasonable living, but looking through some old correspondence, I recalled that we had approached the Council asking for permission to build a crazy golf feature in the most westerly sunken garden on the West Parade, now part of the Drift Park. Our request was not granted, but it reminded me that we were looking for something to supplement our diminishing earnings from the pleasure boat industry.

As early as 1960 we were approached by a boat operator in Fleetwood who wanted to purchase the "May Queen" and at that point in time we had not given any serious thought to selling up, but by 1963, we had to face the grim fact that the deteriorating beach conditions, and the increasing cost of equipment, surveys etc. would make boating unprofitable.

We were by now the sole operator on the beach, Edward Todd had retired, and in 1963 we contacted Tommy Mann, a boat operator in Southport and offered to sell the whole business to him. It turned out that he was only interested in purchasing the boat, and unable to agree a price we carried on, and in 1965 approached another operator in Tenby, offering the boat only this time. Again we were unsuccessful, but the Fleetwood contact was still interested, and seemed to have set his mind on taking the "May Queen" to Fleetwood. Finally after much soul searching, we decided that 1966 would be our last season, and we agreed to sell to him.

I can recall standing on the boat one Autumn day in 1966, looking down the river and realizing my life was about to change for ever, I was sad but also relieved that the uncertainties of each season and the same efforts for less return, were going to be behind me. Also by this time I had a young family, and I looked forward to having a job that gave me more regular hours.

In April 1967, Uncle Stan and I floated the "May Queen" off her winter bed for the last time, prepared her for sea and with the new owner on board, she sailed out of Rhyl for the last time, and I still have a newspaper cutting in which John Povah the well known local boatman and fisherman, mourned the loss of the last of the big passenger vessels to leave Rhyl.

After she had gone, we were approached by Mr. Billy Williams, a long established local amusement operator, who wanted to buy the Packet House and Café, and our workshop, and who offered us a small storage shed in his Quay Street compound.

Having scaled down our activities, we agreed, disposed of our jetties and most of our workshop contents and moved across the road.

We still had the Pearly Monarch speedboat, which my Uncle Stan continued to operate, I had taken on full time work, but assisted at weekends. When he retired in 1972 I bought the boat off him and part exchanged it with Ron Scott of Tarporley, for a Glastron Swinger speedboat, with 80hp. Mercury outboard, capable of carrying seven passengers at thirty knots. Acting on my wife's suggestion I named her "Kool-Kookie", and carried on running trips for some ten years, working only at week-ends, evenings and part of my annual holidays. In 1983 my son Nick and I purchased a steel fishing boat from Grimsby named "Katie Louise" and until 1987 we along with other charter skippers provided angling trips and a very modified version of a trip round the bay. Today 2011, even this attraction has almost ceased to exist.

Now I am retired, and yet some forty four years later I still stand on the promenade and recall the days of crowded beaches, with the pleasure boats bustling in and out, the cries of "anymore for a trip round the bay," and I sometimes imagine I hear the strains of an accordion carried on the breeze.

As for the "May Queen", she stayed in Fleetwood for about three years, and was sold to a company in Falmouth, as referred to in an earlier chapter, where she still plies the ferry to St. Mawes to this day.

ACKNOWLEDGEMENTS

Clwyd Record Office Hawarden for photographs.

Robert Gartside, Canada, for details of his involvement in the passenger boat industry, from 1946-1958

Rev. F.A. Cliff, Rhyl for advice on publishing.

Photographs from family, ex. crew members and friends.

Copyright J. Salmon Ltd. Sevenoaks; The sands from the pier, Rhyl.

The author of this book wishes to confirm that every possible effort has been made to track down and clarify the copyright and ownership of the photographs used.

www.ingramcontent.com/pod-product-compliance
Lightning Source LLC
Chambersburg PA
CBHW071312040426
42444CB00009B/1997